BIGGER
THAN PINK!

The Book I Could Not Find
When I Was Diagnosed
With Stage Four Cancer

by
Lori C. Lober, CSP MIRM
with Lara Moritz

author**HOUSE™**

1663 LIBERTY DRIVE, SUITE 200
BLOOMINGTON, INDIANA 47403
(800) 839-8640
WWW.AUTHORHOUSE.COM

First published by AuthorHouse 01/12/06

ISBN: 1-4184-6150-4 (e)
ISBN: 1-4184-3012-9 (sc)
ISBN: 1-4184-3011-0 (dj)

Library of Congress Control Number: 2004092126

Printed in the United States of America
Bloomington, Indiana

This book is printed on acid-free paper.

For My Beloved Son Colby James McLain
November 21, 1986 - November 28, 2005*
The Angels in Heaven Rejoice to Have You By Their Side

*On November 28, 2005, just prior to publication of this book, Colby McLain
left this world to join God, following a tragic automobile accident. He will
live on forever though in the heart and mind of each person whose life he so
generously and lovingly touched in his brief, but vibrant time on this earth.

For My Brother, Lance Cory Wittmeyer
January, 1965 - May, 2000
You Are My Angel!

Table of Contents

Appendices

Foreword

BY
Larry J. Geier, MD
Medical Oncologist

I first met Lori Lober in 2003 at a symposium focusing on the prevention and early detection of breast cancer. She was one of many women there that day, many of whom were breast cancer survivors. But for some reason she stood out among the crowd, and her questions and comments after my presentation were right on the money and greatly appreciated. We both came away from that encounter with the feeling that, "Gee, he/she really gets what this is all about." I knew that she and others had created the Touched By Cancer Foundation in Kansas City to help current and future cancer patients in a variety of ways, and I sensed in her a level of energy and commitment that I couldn't help but admire. However, I really had no idea until I read this book just how admirable a woman she truly is.

On the surface, the book is an accounting of her trials and tribulations in fighting Stage IV breast cancer, including the things that went wrong, and the things that went right. Since her cancer was invisible to the mammogram, there was an unfortunate delay in her diagnosis. She had difficulty identifying a team of doctors with whom she could communicate in the way that she wanted, and that she could trust would be providing aggressive state-of-the-art care. Ultimately she achieved an amazing result, in that she is cancer-free now, five years out from her diagnosis. That accomplishment is remarkable in itself, no matter what the path to get there.

However, this book is much more than a mere chronicle. It is a window into the person Lori really is, a woman with great spirit, and a remarkable will to survive. She didn't just beat the odds to get where she is today; she refused to accept those odds, and was determined to do whatever it took to give herself the best chance to beat the cancer. This included not only the best and most aggressive therapy that traditional or "Western" medicine had to offer, but also a combination of complementary types of treatment not routinely used in cancer care. Among these were such things as acupuncture, reflexology, herbal medicine, colonic cleansings, and therapeutic touch and massage.

Most of us American-trained physicians know little or nothing about these alternative treatment modalities, and tend to have a certain level of mistrust of them because they don't seem sufficiently "scientific" for our liking. That usually means that we haven't yet figured out a way to measure them scientifically, and thereby "prove" a cause and effect relationship between the treatment and a beneficial outcome. In my opinion, we even tend to be somewhat arrogant in our view, daring to call what we do with surgery and medicines "traditional," while designating treatments that have been used successfully for centuries as "alternative." Some of us are perhaps more open-minded, and prefer to "integrate" the best of both worlds whenever possible, for the maximum benefit of the patient. I certainly don't claim to adequately understand how some of these modalities work, but I have indeed seen them work in many patients…. helping to control pain, to relieve stress, to improve nutritional state, to maintain energy, and to apparently bolster the immune system. I honestly don't know if they help to fight the cancer directly in some way we can't yet define, but I know all too well the limitations of chemotherapy, radiation, and surgery, and frankly, I can use all the help I can get. I do prefer to know when my patients are considering such therapies so that I can help to guide them the best I can, but I know I still have much to learn. To that end, this book has been quite helpful, and I have learned much from Lori's descriptions of the various treatments she included in her program, why she chose them, and the benefits she received. It might be that a different combination would be effective in different patients, but these are surely a good place to start.

Presumably you are reading this book because either you or someone you care about is battling cancer. If so, I believe you will find it to be both instructional and inspirational, a rare combination. Lori alludes to Lance Armstrong and how she found his book to be inspirational to her, but I believe if their positions were reversed, he would say the same thing about her writings. Lori once asked me if I thought she was truly a "cancer survivor" since she had Stage IV disease and is still taking active therapy. No one can say for sure whether she is truly "cured" or is living in harmony with her disease, but it is certainly true that for some people cancer is best viewed as a chronic illness requiring chronic management. Either way, in my view Lori is the absolute personification of the phrase cancer survivor. I find her spirit and determination, her ability to integrate the best of traditional and alternative medicine, tailored to her own needs, and her willingness to give to others without hesitation, all to be remarkable, admirable, and truly inspiring.

Larry J. Geier, MD
Medical Oncologist

Lori Lober, © 2004 Robert Schlatter

Note From the Author

In April 2000, I was diagnosed with Stage IV metastatic breast cancer. At that defining moment I made a decision that would impact the rest of my life: I would live whatever life I had left as positively as I could. Even after my double-mastectomy (with no reconstruction), when I caught the image of myself in the mirror each morning, I chose to see the scar that runs from my left armpit to my right armpit, as a smile. This perception serves as a reminder of what I have been through and what has made me the person I am today. If I had not made that conscious decision I might be overwhelmed with sorrow and embarrassment because of how my body now looks. Battling cancer reminded me that outward appearance is unimportant – that it's what is inside your heart and mind, how you treat others, and ultimately, your self-respect, that truly matters most. My diagnosis forced me to slow down and exit the "fast track". Now, every day is special and friendships are more meaningful. I have never been happier in my life. This alone has convinced me that being diagnosed with advanced stage cancer, for me, was more than a "wake up call", it was a gift from God. The blessings that I have received have brought me an ever-present joy that has carried me through adversity, as if a gentle breeze were sending me adrift like a feather; reminding me that my path leads to greater meaning and love, happiness and joy.

It is now 2005. Five years ago I had less than a 5% chance of survival, yet I am alive and well with no evidence of disease in my body. Perhaps, the only real fact that we can hold true is that while death is inevitable, life is a gift which we cannot explain with absolute certainty. What I do know is that I have the power to live the way I choose and to choose the way I live. The beauty of life is that it has no limits, only endless opportunities at each crossroad, where meaning can be experienced through love and love can filter through life. God Bless.

Introduction

Who am I and why am I writing this book? The answer to the first part of this question is fairly straightforward. My name is Lori Lober, I live in Kansas City, Missouri, and work alongside my husband John in the home-building industry. I am a wife, a mother, and a Stage IV cancer survivor. The answer to the latter part of this question is a bit more complex. There seems to be no shortage of books about cancer and terminal cancer patients. In April 2000 when I was diagnosed with breast cancer, I searched everywhere for hope and help – for a better understanding of my illness and ways in which I could combat it. I read everything I could get my hands on.

I encountered stories of triumph and inspiration. Richard Bloch's story was a great one. The fact that he was from my hometown helped somewhat, and I know he helped many cancer patients. However, my greatest source of inspiration came in the Spring of 2002 when I read Lance Armstrong's book, *"It's Not About the Bike"* (if you have not read it, I highly recommend it, regardless of whether or not you are fighting cancer). Reading about Lance and his struggles and ultimate success battling cancer, gave me hope (although I did not have it when I truly needed it – if only I had his book sooner!). Lance Armstrong, in my mind, is "super-human", and by learning of his strengths, extraordinary gifts, and successes, I found my own strength. He has served as my hero and inspiration.

Unfortunately, these stories were more the exception than the rule. Much of the information I found seemed to be either out-dated or "far-out". Many of us have seen and heard of the crazy ways some believe cancer can be cured. I even read about how drinking my own urine would cure me! I continued searching. I read numerous stories, books, and articles written by cancer patients – many of whom ultimately died. This naturally depressed me, leaving me with more questions than answers. Witnessing my younger brother's battle with cancer had taught me that my own life now depended on being proactive. It was time to take matters into my own hands.

After my diagnosis, I began pre-operative chemotherapy ("chemo") immediately. Once I became comfortable with the multi-disciplinary team of physicians at M.D. Anderson Cancer Center (MDACC) in Houston, Texas, I felt totally confident that my recommended course of treatment would offer the best chance for long term survival. First, five months of pre-operative chemo was necessary to shrink the tumors as much as possible, since the cancer had already spread throughout my lymphatic system and I also had two tumors in my liver. Three months later, the liver tumors were shrinking. In September 2000, I underwent an experimental surgery called radio-frequency ablation. The physicians explained that rather than performing surgery, ultrasound-guided radiated therapy to the tumor would offer me greater hope. The team at MDACC believed it was a success, but only time would tell. (Over five years later, I now hear what was then an experimental procedure, referred to as a mainstream treatment option). After a three-week "vacation" from chemo, I underwent another cycle just prior to undergoing a double-mastectomy in November 2000.

One does not die from cancer that is confined to the breast(s), but rather, it's only after cancer has spread throughout the lymphatic system and forms distant tumors in other critical parts of the body (e.g. the liver, brain, lungs or bones) that it can kill you. I mention this because throughout my journey, especially in the beginning, many reassured me: "you'll be ok". They believed this because it seemed as though everyone knew someone who had breast cancer five, ten or even twenty years ago and "they're still doing great!" It was only after I would ask these same people that if, in fact, the cancer had metastasized (spread), most had to confess they were uncertain.

While I was confident about the treatment I was receiving at MDACC, I continued to search for what seemed to be good ideas or additional modalities I could incorporate with my prescribed traditional, "Western" treatments. Beginning in April 2000, beating cancer became my full-time job. At this point, nothing was more deserving of my time and energy. My chemotherapy treatments continued, and I devoted one full day each week to that. Throughout my journey (and believe me, it's not over) I have incorporated several complementary treatments. Based on my research and reading, I began to receive therapeutic massage every Tuesday, acupuncture on Monday, Wednesday and Friday, and reflexology on Thursday. I also traveled to M.D. Anderson Cancer Center monthly as well. This was necessary since I was participating in a clinical trial. As you can see, I was very busy. I believe that this was ultimately very beneficial to me, since it left precious little time to feel sorry for myself.

On January 1, 2001 (01-01-01 --- a sign?), while feeling poorly from the chemo, together with my husband John, I stumbled across *Dateline*, the NBC television show. The entire hour was dedicated to the story of Dr. Yeshi Dhonden, a Tibetan monk who specializes in treating metastatic breast cancer. He had also been the personal physician to the Dalai Lama for over twenty years. Dr. Dhonden comes to the United States twice a year from Dharamsala, India. I felt I had to see him and I did. I've been a regular patient of his since October 2001. I have taken Tibetan herbs recommended by Dr. Dhonden, three times each day since then. As a matter of fact, it was Dr. Dhonden, my Eastern medicine physician, who first declared that there was no cancer in my body during that first visit! (His pronouncement was confirmed by my "Western" medicine physicians shortly thereafter). Of course, we discussed diet, exercise, herbal supplementation and many other things. I would need to continue to do "everything right" for a very, very long time in order to keep the cancer from "wanting" to invade my body ever again.

I continued chemotherapy as well. My acupuncturist told me he was going to prescribe Shou Wu Wan, a blend of Chinese herbs, to make my hair start growing back. I thought we were experiencing a breakdown in communication. I said, "No, you don't understand. I am going to continue receiving chemotherapy for a long, long time". He replied, "No, I do understand. In spite of the continual chemo, I am going to make your hair start to come back." I bought the herb, I took it and my hair began to come back. (It was great having my own hair when, my husband John and I renewed our marriage vows at the height of my chemotherapy treatments!) I still think my oncologist was a little freaked out each month I saw him at MDACC—the Stage IV bald lady from Kansas City had hair!

I turned forty years old October 31, 2003. In 2000, my odds of seeing my fortieth birthday were very slim (2-3% chance of survival, at best). So, it truly was a milestone for me, my family, and friends! I'll always remember my "spa trip" to celebrate with some of my closest friends, and my surprise birthday party with many dear friends present!

I am now celebrating 2005. The last five years of my life have been spent fighting cancer. However, my fight goes on. I continue to receive a chemotherapeutic antibody (Herceptin) on a regular basis. (It does not kill fast-growing cells like hair). In total, I received Taxotere/Herceptin in combination for seven months, Adriamycin, Cytoxin, 5-FU and Navelbene for four months each. I have undergone six surgical procedures (two eye surgeries were needed because of increased tearing from all the chemo) and an unbelievable amount of tests, physicians' appointments, as well as a wide variety of wellness appointments.

This brings us back to why I am writing this book. I simply want to help as many people whose lives have been affected by cancer, as I possibly can. I made a promise to God to do so, when I first realized the gravity of my diagnosis – before, during and after each periodic test I undergo to determine whether or not the cancer has returned, I have reaffirmed that promise.

I'm telling my story with the hope that it will make someone else's journey easier. I spend many hours every week telling my story to patients, their friends and loved ones. I have spent countless hours at luncheons, dinners, and other functions/fund-raisers, conversing with fellow cancer patients. I have found that they are all hungry for information, guidance and a real-life success story. Perhaps I can be that success story and convince other cancer patients to seek out all their options. I am not a medical doctor. I have received no formal training of any kind relating to medicine or health. I am, however, a fighter. I'm an ordinary person who has made beating cancer my long-term goal and thus far I'm alive and well. Is it the chemotherapy? Is the Herceptin I continue to receive keeping the HER-2 NEU (the oncogene that fed my very aggressive tumor) in check? Have the 100+ herbs, vitamins and supplements I take regularly played a role? Has drinking green (or red or white) tea regularly and eating only fruit each morning been a factor? Has my unwavering faith in God and my continual meditation played a role? My physicians cannot tell me for certain. However, I will give you an honest account of my journey and if this little book can help even one person beat cancer, one of my dreams will have been fulfilled and I'll be tickled pink!

Chapter 1

The Power that Lies Within

"I saw myself as whole and well on the other side of my treatments."

In April 2000 when I was diagnosed with Stage IV breast cancer, I went through a period of shock that produced many mixed thoughts and emotions. Most of my thoughts caused me to worry, and most of my worries caused me to fear. It is important to understand that these feelings are normal for a newly-diagnosed cancer patient. At first, such feelings may seem negative, but they can be channeled into positive feelings and a positive attitude. If you are about to become a "world champ fighter", jumping in the ring with the fiercest of opponents (cancer!), then a positive outlook is the best of allies.

I began to view my worries and fears as the fuel that would ignite determination, intuition, work ethic, and conviction. I worried about what would happen to my family and friends if I was no longer there for them. I also worried about how and where I would die and in what manner I would be put to rest. I actually began to plan my funeral. I visited a psychologist, and she explained that it was very healthy and natural for me to be experiencing these thoughts and feelings under the circumstances. At first, I had a difficult time understanding how this could be healthy. Then I realized I was simply afraid of dying. I began facing my fear of death. It was human nature for me to worry that I was going to die, but recognizing and confronting my fear helped me to arrive at a greater and beneficial understanding: *everyone dies at some point, but there isn't anyone on this earth that can predict exactly how long I have to live*. Cancer can certainly be life-threatening, but it does not necessarily have to be life-ending. I understood, embraced, and believed in the possibility that I might survive. I turned worry and fear into hope and belief, which then enabled me to develop a positive outlook. I was then able to channel hopelessness into constructive thoughts that would help me find and focus on a path to recovery. Positive thinking will provide the foundation for inspiration and guidance, to always stay the course and to never give up. Understand that negative and even heart-breaking news can fuel you throughout your struggle to beat cancer. I realized that even the most hopeless situation can be reversed and transformed into power. Hopelessness can be countered by conviction, control and the realization that the mind is extremely powerful and sometimes it is possible to achieve the seemingly unimaginable.

"*Cancer wants to kill me*". I had to put this thought out of my mind. If I allowed it to take over my emotions and attitudes, then it could weaken my resolve, and be a drain on the "fuel reserves" I was building. Cancer is an obstacle that often seems overwhelming and impossible to overcome, but I firmly believed that I was strong enough to do so. I saw myself as whole and well on the other side of my treatments. I visualized my physician saying, appointment after appointment, "You have no cancer in your body."

Hopelessness does not exist in the mind of a positive thinker, so I got rid of it. Instead, I came to realize how in control of my life I could be, regardless of the presence of cancer in my body. The daily reality of living with and fighting cancer offered little hope, but taking control and becoming determined to live and live well, filled my heart with hope. I persistently searched my soul for every ounce of belief that I could muster. Every minute, every hour and every day became opportunities to live, learn, and grow as a wife, mother, sister, and as a cancer patient. I learned that when we can clear our Qi —our emotional body — of counter-productive and life-distorting matter and emotions, healing is accelerated and life becomes more purposeful, joyful, and fulfilling.

When I heard the words, "*you have cancer*", my life seemed to crumble before me. I was thirty-four years old when I first found the suspicious lump in my breast. Following a mammogram, I was told not to worry, that it was only fibrocystic disease, which approximately 75% of women are diagnosed with at some point. Needless to say, I was relieved to hear that it was something that was supposedly very common and treatable. But for the next two years, the lump grew larger, and the pain surrounding it, although not always present, became more intense. Yet deep inside, I knew something was wrong. I didn't obsess about it, but I did think about it often despite several more trips to the doctor, mammograms, and breast exams, the results of which were all negative.

In spite of that nagging feeling I had that something was very wrong, my eventual diagnosis (metastatic breast cancer that had progressed to the most severe stage), was still an incredible shock to me. Cancer had spread throughout my lymphatic system and to my liver. My husband John and I could not believe what we were hearing. The results of a mammogram just one week prior to the diagnosis, indicated "no sign of cancer – please return for another mammogram at age forty" (that would be in another four years). I was angry, for I could not understand how both mammograms and physicians' breast exams could not produce a timely and correct diagnosis. I had been misdiagnosed for two years during which time the cancer had progressed to the most terminal and severe stage of metastasis. I was given an estimated eighteen months to live; a two to three percent survival rate, at this stage.

My misdiagnosis and statistically poor chance of survival, left me with little hope and waning confidence in conventional medicine alone. I read every book I could possibly find on the topic, and most left me sad and listless. Things were not turning out the way they were supposed to. However, herein is a perfect illustration of the power of positive thinking! I was angry with the doctors. I was angry that three mammograms failed to detect the cancer, when, in fact, my breast tumor was almost the size of an egg. I nearly allowed my anger to negatively affect my opinions about doctors and conventional Western medicine in general. This most definitely would have been the wrong path to take. In my opinion, and I believe most would agree, conventional Western medicine is essential in the treatment and survival of cancer. Harboring negative thoughts and beliefs during my search for the best conventional treatment could influence my decision-making and lead to an overall poor result. So I chose to redirect my inner energies away from anger and disbelief, and toward a useful, productive and action-oriented state of mind. Consequently, I considered the end of my two-year period of misdiagnosis as a call to action. It was time for me to take control of my treatment plan, and I now felt that my survival was largely up to me.

There are many physicians who treat cancer daily, but naturally, there is no one more focused on my survival than me. At this point I knew that I had to find a Comprehensive Cancer Center and a treatment team that would be working *for* me and not *on* me. I knew that I needed to get the ball rolling since according to statistics, I had, after all, relatively little time.

Affirmations and Angels. I will admit, it was extremely challenging for me to draw anything positive from the unpromising statistics of my diagnosis. Physicians clearly conveyed the message that I was most likely going to die sooner rather than later. Therefore, I decided to acknowledge the statistics as a reminder of the significance that I must play in my survival. I jumped into the ring and starting fighting. I became highly competitive in proving the statistics wrong. I was not a statistic and I refused to become one!

I used affirmations in order to continually empower myself and remain motivated. I would say them aloud and to myself throughout each day, especially when I felt that my positive thinking was being challenged. (Although I now have no evidence of disease in my body, I continue to do this daily). This is another method I used to remain focused on the path to recovery.

One must control one's mind, then the mind can control the body — this was my mantra. I thought, "Lori, if you are constantly thinking negative thoughts you will have a negative attitude. You are a human being with a powerful mind, body, and spirit. You are capable of overcoming anything!" I would assert that "my body is whole and well" or "my body is happy, healthy and whole" every morning when I would wake up and every night when I went to bed. I also made these assertions whenever I had a few free moments to meditate — waiting at various appointments, while undergoing scans and x-rays — every extra little bit of time I could find. Even when I visited the bathroom I would envision the cancer being flushed down the toilet!

I gave continual thanks daily for all that I had to feel happy about: my marriage, my wonderful son, great family and friends! Now my gratitude is also for simpler pleasures, like being able to witness the sunshine glisten off the snow on a winter's morning, as if God Himself was telling me "everything is fine." Perhaps we are too often distracted by the rigors of our daily lives to notice when God is trying to remind us that He is there, He is watching and we are important. In graciousness, we let God know that we believe and in our belief we find purpose. My world before cancer had never been this beautiful. It is amazing how my senses came alive after being diagnosed with a life-threatening illness! I remember when I took such great pride in being a career woman, firmly on the path to bigger and better things in the new home-building business, and the great importance I placed on those goals — that all seems so distant now.

I have a strong belief in the presence of angels among us here on Earth. The image of an angel with wings hovering above those in need, comforts me. In the depths of my battle against cancer, I came to believe that God would place a white feather from the wings of an angel for me to see, so I would continue to believe in the purposeful beauty of my life.

God has filled my soul with hope in the representation of a white feather, many times. This first occurred while on a vacation in Jamaica following three months of exhausting chemotherapy in the summer of 2002. On this trip I read Lance Armstrong's book, *"It's Not About the Bike"* which brought me great hope, and reaffirmed my belief in my survival. I later flew back home to the U.S. thinking of the story of Lance's triumph over cancer.

At one point during the trip, a good friend and I stopped to pose for a photo in a garden overlooking the beautiful Caribbean Ocean. I felt so connected to Lance's book that I clutched it and held it close to me while the photo was taken. Afterwards, we looked down and saw a white feather lying between us at our feet. We glanced up and noticed that there was not a single bird in the sky. Somehow, this seemingly insignificant event touched me with an overwhelming sense of meaning. It gave me a feeling of strength which reinforced my belief, the recognition of a friend who supports my belief, and a God who believes in me.

I believe that if you keep a watchful eye, then you will find moments such as these every day. Pay attention to everything that brings you joy and then give thanks. If you find reasons to be thankful for life, you will find strength to face the adversity that challenges you. Find reasons to live. Recognize the blessings that have been bestowed upon you and use these gifts as reminders of why you want to live.

The struggle to beat cancer was an emotional roller coaster for me. I could not avoid having negative emotions, but I did refuse to allow them to consume me. I conquered them with my desire to live. Every feeling, emotion and experience in life happens for a reason. The future is determined by how one chooses to deal with them. I used affirmations; I prayed, gave thanks and I converted every experience into positive energy. I was going to do whatever it took to survive.

From Resolve to Action. In the summer of 2002, I was finally sure of myself. I had received a bundle of awful news, and I managed to overcome my negativity and create positive energy. I had developed conviction and a resolve to win the fight, which was a result of knowledge and understanding. With strong conviction and belief, I was able to be courageous and take action – nothing heroic mind you, but acting upon my conviction without fear of failure. I channeled my actions in a positive way to underscore and support my beliefs.

In addition to positive thinking, I found that an action-oriented attitude and focus is required in the fight against cancer. Survival must now be my number one priority. I could no longer worry about the house being dusty, the laundry piling up, the kids' next baseball practice. I now focused on *me* – in the short-term, on survival, in the longer-term, on living a long, healthy and fulfilling life! In the long run, life's everyday, mundane chores will not be a concern, so I set those aside. Other, generally more important concerns that may include family, career, economics, while more difficult, would also have to become secondary.

The moment I began to take a proactive stance toward my treatment and recovery was when I truly developed a strong sense of self-determination and control over my destiny. I focused every ounce of energy that I possessed into gathering information and learning in order to ensure I was making sound decisions. I bought books and literature, searched the internet, asked my physicians countless questions and constantly requested information of them (I'm certain I was driving them crazy!) I asked for charts, graphs, explanations, and recommendations. I insisted that my physicians make any medical jargon understandable to me. If I was to choose among various treatments, I would make certain that I knew exactly the potential demands (of me) and benefits of each, before moving forward. I needed to be confident that the treatment would result in progress. I was an active participant in my treatment program. I felt in charge, but yet still had much to do.

During my research I stumbled upon other potentially beneficial, albeit somewhat "different" forms of treatment. I found that I could integrate complementary modalities into my treatment plan and that each may play an important role in my long-term survival. I began to incorporate acupuncture, reflexology, colonics, proper nutrition, Eastern herbal medicine, and therapeutic massage. These treatments helped to relieve the side effects of chemotherapy, strengthen my immune system, and perhaps most importantly, relieve stress. I firmly believe that the integration of these modalities with conventional medicine is essential for recovery, as they all contribute to strengthening body and mind alike. If it had not been for my active research, I would never have considered any of these treatments. After doing so, I realized how important it can be to keep an open mind and consider all available options, when searching for the best cancer treatment plan. My personal, integrated treatment plan may not necessarily be what is best for everyone, but I believe that exploring all options is vitally important (and should be driven by that action-oriented attitude!) An open-minded approach can support the overall wellness of the mind, body, and spirit, which I believe can materially improve the chances of recovery and survival.

Positive thinking can help to achieve wellness, and an active approach to treatment which includes exhausting all options, can dramatically increase the chances of survival. Optimism and action go hand in hand in the battle against cancer. No matter how severe the diagnosis, I believe that recovery from cancer is a much stronger possibility if the patient marshals his/her inner power to think positively and to truly believe that everything he/she is doing to "beat cancer" in combination is, in fact, working.

Cancer is not necessarily a death sentence. Whether cancer is discovered in its early stages, or has progressed to Stage IV, it is important to understand that the diagnosis is like being handed a road map of your future life — you need to study it and decide where and how you want to travel.

I have known and loved several strong individuals that sadly, have died from cancer. In contrast, there are also many cancer survivors — more and more each year. I am an ordinary person and I have survived the most terminal stage of breast cancer. I believe that we all possess the inner strength to fight cancer, and that God does not place challenges before us that He has not equipped us to handle. We all have the potential to harness that strength in order to face and overcome the obstacles that we encounter in our lives. If I can do it, then you can too!

Chapter 2

The Power of Early Diagnosis and Multiple Opinions

"Question the doctor – the lesson for a patient is to ask your doctor about treatment options, why they would or would not apply, and why a certain treatment is being recommended. Then, get another opinion from another type of doctor such as a urologist or radiologist who specializes…. and ask the same questions."

Hollister H. Hovey. "Too Quick To Cut."
The Wall Street Journal December 9, 2003

As mentioned in the previous chapter, a main component of an action-oriented attitude is an open mind that explores all options. Early detection and diagnosis, and multiple opinions will direct and position you on a path of action.

This chapter will address a number of early warning signs that could help avoid cancer before it emerges or detect it in its earliest stages. Education can provide opportunities to recognize some early signs of cancer that could present as a painful lump in your breast, a chronic cough or a persistent watery eye. It could also possibly enable you to help another who is curious or worried about an irregularity or radical change in their health. Whether a friend, loved one, or acquaintance, you may be able to notice various indicators and advise on the importance of immediate examination by a physician. And, learning what the early signs are will help you better understand your own body's status.

Acquiring a second, and possibly third opinion, is often a key factor in the survival of cancer. This chapter will explain the approach that I believe is the most productive based on my research and personal experience. It will address why multiple opinions are important and how to go about obtaining them.

Early Warning Signs and Detection. There are clinical procedures that can identify cancer: blood tests, mammograms, x-rays, physical examinations, biopsies, etc. Many of these methods will indicate whether or not cancer is a possibility. However, personal awareness of your body and its overall wellness and recognition of the signs it sends you, can be a powerful weapon in the battle against cancer. Understand that you are the most valuable asset to every endeavor in that battle. In my case, I was assured that there was no evidence of cancer in my body. However, not only did I have an egg-sized tumor in my breast, the cancer had spread throughout my lymphatic system and I had two tumors in my liver. If I had not persistently "listened" to what my body was "telling me" via the signs it was sending, then without a doubt, I would not be alive today.

Pay close attention to your body; it's constantly trying to make you aware of its status. The National Cancer Institute website lists a sampling of a wide variety of symptoms that cancer can cause, including:

- Thickening or lump in the breast or any other part of the body
- Obvious change in a wart or mole
- A sore that does not heal
- Nagging cough or hoarseness
- Changes in bowel or bladder habits
- Indigestion or difficulty swallowing
- Unexplained changes in weight
- Unusual bleeding or discharge

The site goes on to point out that when these symptoms occur, they are not always caused by cancer. They may also be signs of infections, benign tumors, or other problems. The point is, it is important not to ignore what your body is telling you and to see a doctor soon. One should not wait, as cancer in its early stages, often does not cause pain.

Diagnostic Methods and Potential Shortcomings. For the most part, conventional detection is effective but there are certain situations that have produced inaccurate results. Blood tests are one example. This form of detection is often successful but is not perfect. Blood tests are most beneficial in pinpointing the progression or regression of cancer, but have a tendency to distinguish material that is unrelated (to cancer) or caused by an entirely different condition.

This creates the possibility of a positive cancer diagnosis when it should be negative. Conversely, there is also the danger of a negative diagnosis when in fact, cancer is present. In fact, at the time of my diagnosis, my CA27.29 test fell within normal limits. This is a blood test that measures a particular substance that cancer cells secrete into the bloodstream. Some normal cells also make up this substance, and some breast cancer cells do not secrete it at all. This was the case in my situation. Obviously, believing that you do not have cancer, when you actually do, can be fatal.

An incorrect diagnosis can also be made based on mammogram results. Typically, the breasts of women under age forty are denser than the breasts of older women. This makes it more difficult for mammograms to consistently detect cancer across women of all age groups. I discovered this the hard way. I wish I had known this when I had my first mammogram at age thirty-four. I believe this is one of the main reasons for my misdiagnosis. Fortunately, persistence led me to a more precise method of detection.

Two years later, I received a proper diagnosis through biopsy. The only sure way to diagnose breast cancer is a biopsy. Other procedures simply hint at the possibility of cancer. In spite of this, a biopsy is not 100% accurate, even if it is the most effective diagnostic method. According to Colonel Craig Shriver, M.D., F.A.C.S., M.C., Director and Principal Investigator - Clinical Breast Care Project, Program Director and Chief - General Surgery Service of Walter Reed Army Medical Center, and Associate Professor of Surgery for the Uniformed Services University, "Eighty percent of all biopsies are negative, meaning they are benign or non-cancerous. If, in fact, a biopsy comes back positive, in my opinion, once diagnosed with breast cancer, even if non-invasive, the patient should obtain an opinion or evaluation at a comprehensive cancer center at that point. There are studies in medical literature supporting improved cancer survival outcomes, at certain "Centers of Excellence", especially for complex types of cancers or when multi-disciplinary treatment is given. These are very strictly defined organizations that are designated by the

National Cancer Institute as having expertise in various types of cancers with regard to clinical and basic scientific research. This has been clearly shown for breast cancer, pancreatic cancer and rectal cancer."

Colonel Shriver also suggests one visit www.oncolink.com, as it is very user-friendly and under constant peer review. He goes on to add, "It does not allow links or information that does not meet rigorous standards that most medical professionals desire. This site does the homework for the patients and should certainly be regarded as being the best information available."

Keep in mind that the diagnosis is only as good as the pathologist. Pathology is the medical specialty that reviews and studies biopsies to determine proper diagnosis. The pathologist's level of expertise is a key factor in the success of the procedure, so be certain to locate a Board-certified pathologist, specializing in oncology. The National Cancer Institute does rate and set strict criteria with regard to cancer centers and their "approved" physicians. According to Col. Shriver, the two best sources for obtaining this information are the National Cancer Institute website, www.nationalcancerinstitute.com, and also at the same site, one could research "SPORE" also known as "Specialized Program of Research Excellence" sites.

Multiple Opinions. The horrifying words *"you have cancer"* have a tendency to cause panic. These thoughts manifest in the hours and days following your diagnosis. Do not let them control your actions. You will need a clear head in order to obtain multiple opinions, and you should not attempt to do so in desperation or haste. A useful fact about cancer is that in most cases there is a sufficient amount of time following diagnosis to organize a qualified treatment team and a treatment program. The plan starts in your mind with positive thinking, and execution of the plan begins with acquiring a second and possibly third medical opinion.

A *Wall Street Journal* article by Hollister H. Hovey, dated December 9, 2003, states "More than 200,000 men will be diagnosed with prostate cancer in the U.S. this year, but despite a number of treatment options, many men will undergo radical prostatectomies without considering other, less invasive procedures that might be just as effective." The article goes on to point out that one reason men diagnosed with prostate cancer don't learn of other options, is that many are often first referred to surgeons, whereas many newer treatments are performed by other doctors such as urologists, radiologists or oncologists who specialize in prostate malignancies.

"Doctors have a great tendency toward *'you've got cancer, take it out'*", says Peter Scardino, a surgeon and Chairman of the Department of Urology at New York's Memorial Sloan-Kettering Cancer Center.

I first learned the importance of this when I witnessed my brother Lance fight cancer. He was misdiagnosed for three years before he died of cancer at the young age of thirty-five. Lance was first diagnosed with a rare form of sarcoma. Chemotherapy was not effective for this type of cancer, so his physicians opted to surgically remove his tumors on four different occasions. Each time, the tumors returned. After a few years, a family friend suggested we consult with a team of physicians at M.D. Anderson Cancer Center in Houston, Texas. We had no knowledge of this facility, nor did we know what a comprehensive cancer center was. Within the first forty-eight hours there, we were told that Lance had a totally different kind of cancer — one that was generally very receptive to chemotherapy. Unfortunately, it was too late and my brother could not be saved.

While Lance's death was dreadfully hard to endure, it provided me with an experiential understanding that multiple pathology opinions are an absolute necessity. If not for Lance, I might have accepted my initial diagnosis and I would probably be dead now.

Obtaining multiple opinions is literally that important. While some may see this as directly questioning or challenging a physician's professional judgment, it is not — it is simply verifying the diagnosis and comparing more than one point of view. When it comes to life or death, forget about offending your physician. You need to find the best team of physicians to help you fight your cancer. That needs to become your new full-time job! You need to see one, two, even three physicians before you settle on a treatment plan. If two opinions match, you may have the facts you need to make a sound decision. If for any reason you don't feel 100% comfortable with what a physician is proposing, then obtain yet another opinion. It's your life.

Staging and Grading of Cancer. Staging or grading of cancer requires a series of examinations and testing which are conducted in order to learn the extent of the cancer. The same *Wall Street Journal* article quoted previously, also states, "Although the initial diagnosis of prostate cancer is generally correct, about 20% of the time, mistakes are made in the staging and grading of the cancer, according to a review of thousands of second opinions issued by researchers at Johns Hopkins School of Medicine in Baltimore."

While the focus of this article is prostate cancer, it underscores the importance of second opinions not only to determine the exact type of cancer, but also the extent of cancer in the body.

Staging of cancer is described by the NCI as "performing exams and tests to learn the extent of the cancer within the body, especially whether the disease has spread from the original site to other parts of the body. It is important to know the stage of the disease in order to plan the best treatment." For further information on staging and grading of cancer, visit the National Cancer Institute's website at www.nci.nih.gov.

Choosing Your Physician(s). First, locate and consult a Board-certified oncologist before undergoing any surgery. According to HealthGrades.com, "Board certified physicians have completed extensive training and testing, going above and beyond medical practice licensure. Each medical specialty has a national Board responsible for setting standards that physicians must meet in order to be certified. Board certified physicians have completed several years of training beyond medical school, have practiced for a designated number of years in that specialty, and have passed examinations in their specialty area. Once certified, physicians must attend continuing medical education programs throughout their careers in order to remain certified. Some physicians have more than one Board certification."

Dr. Shriver further clarifies: "Board-certification refers to a physician who has taken all the required training, and passed all of the rigorous requirements of the Hematology-Oncology Boards of the American Board of Medical Specialties (this applies only to Medical Oncologists in this regard). Surgical Oncologists should have completed training in a Society of Surgical Oncology-approved Fellowship Training Program, as there are no Boards available at this time for Surgical Oncologists."

Obviously, there is a significant difference between an oncologist and a general practitioner physician. An oncologist specializes in the treatment of cancer, and has received specialized, in-depth education and training, and will therefore have a greater understanding of what to expect from a given cancer diagnosis. A general practitioner is trained to treat a number of illnesses such as influenza, broken bones, sprains, separations, dislocations, fever, infection, etc. This type of practice requires a broad education of various types of illness and injury that is not typically concentrated in any one area such as cancer. You most certainly want a physician trained to recognize and treat your particular disease. Again, in my opinion, it is crucial that you meet with an oncologist *prior* to undergoing any surgery.

Next, simply be aware that many physicians are connected to one another in a variety of ways. Subsequent opinions should not be impacted by a previous one. My research made it apparent that there is the possibility of a physician simply agreeing with a preceding opinion. I believe this is done to avoid conflict with another physician so as not to compromise his/her professional opinion. In order to prevent this from happening, search for an oncologist who is not associated with the initial or former treating physician. It is likely easier to secure independent, unbiased opinions, if obtained at entirely different hospitals, even in different cities or states. If possible, try to avoid informing the oncologist of the original diagnosis or previous method of treatment until after his/her opinion has been provided. These steps will provide an unbiased point of view that can be more easily compared to other opinions.

While consulting a Board-certified oncologist helps to ensure you access to a high level of expertise, it is also important for you to know the extent of his/her qualifications. Check his/her credentials. Ask what college and medical school he/she attended. Does he/she have knowledge of and access to clinical and experimental trials? Inquire about the extent of experience in the field of patient care in addition to that of his/her associates. When you choose an oncologist, they will be your partner throughout your cancer journey, so make certain you are confident in his/her abilities.

I obtained second and third opinions before making my final decision regarding which physicians to work with. I selected a multi-disciplinary team of physicians at M.D. Anderson Cancer Center in Houston, Texas. My oncologist, the pathologist, the team of surgeons (breast, liver and eye) and the radiologist, all consulted with one another and with me, after reviewing all the tests and scans. This team of professionals informed and educated me about all of my options. As a team, they concluded that pre-operative chemotherapy offered me the greatest hope for survival. I felt comfortable with their level of combined expertise. The time and effort I invested searching for this team, was well worth it.

Developing a Partnership With Your Physician. Your physician's communication skills can help you detect whether he/she will truly care and tend to your needs. The way he/she communicates with you and your family, can provide insight as to whether you are viewed as a patient or a project. You are entitled to a physician who attempts to build a relationship with you and considers your feelings and input important.

I recall a particular appointment in the very beginning of my journey when my husband and I went together to obtain another opinion. The physician explained to us that although he was sure my condition was nothing to be concerned about, he would have to perform a biopsy to confirm that. It was encouraging that he was willing to take this precaution. However, when we asked if this procedure would leave a scar, he replied "yes" in a rude and demeaning tone of voice. We then asked if perhaps he could perform the procedure in such a way as to inflict a less noticeable scar, and he answered very rudely "NO!" We then felt silly for asking the question. On the way home, my husband and I discussed the physician's attitude and decided that it would be best to seek yet another opinion from another physician before making our final decision. Bedside manner and how comfortable you feel during visits, are very important when choosing your medical team.

Ensure the physician uses language that you and your family can understand. Does he/she make you aware of your options and take the time to help you understand them? Is your physician listening to your questions and willing to take the time to answer them? Does he/she ask you if what they've said is clear? Does your physician seem rushed and unfocused or attentive and caring? Is he/she making you aware of the fact that there are clinical trials underway for nearly all types of cancer? Beginning chemotherapy prior to ruling out all possible clinical trials that you may be eligible for, could be a mistake. I was told that traditional chemotherapy would most likely be of no benefit to me at my Stage IV diagnosis. Instead, my lead oncologist at M.D. Anderson Cancer Center (and my MDACC team), highly recommended an experimental chemotherapy regime – one which they felt offered more hope. Had I opted for the traditional chemotherapy, it may have disqualified me from being accepted into the experimental protocol. To this day, I feel blessed that I was able to participate in the Taxotere/Herceptin clinical trial in May of 2000. Five years later, I continue to receive Herceptin infusions, a drug developed by leading biotechnology research firm, Genentech, Inc., specifically for metastatic breast cancer in HER2 overexpressed tumors (for more information visit www.gene.com). It could be one of the reasons I am alive and well today!

Financial Considerations. Obtaining multiple opinions can be expensive. Insurance often does not cover all charges in this category.

Do not allow financial considerations to hinder your chances of long-term survival. If money is a concern, seek a non-profit cancer foundation that can help guide you. Do some research – be proactive – you never know what you might find. For example, I found that it is possible to receive social security disability income if you have been diagnosed with (Stage IV) cancer. If this is true in your case, you are most likely entitled to these funds. The logic underlying provision of these benefits is that the Social Security Administration considers anyone diagnosed with life-threatening illnesses to be entitled to the funds they have paid in to the system over the years now, given the fact they probably will not live to retirement age. I urge you to research this possibility. It may prove to be of considerable financial assistance and help enable you to go wherever you need to in order to receive the best possible treatment.

The Multi-Disciplinary Treatment Approach. I went to a "Comprehensive Cancer Center". As discussed earlier, unfortunately, my family and I did not learn about Comprehensive Cancer Centers during my brother's battle with cancer, until it was too late. Of course, we would have brought him to Houston sooner had we known. I found that many of the best physicians are hired by facilities that have an outstanding reputation. Comprehensive Cancer Centers such as M.D. Anderson in Houston, only accept physicians with specialized expertise in the field of cancer. These physicians treat hundreds of cancer patients every month as opposed to every year. Another important attribute of Comprehensive Cancer Centers was explained to me during my interview with my lead oncologist at M.D. Anderson. He said, "One of the advantages that we have here is our multi-disciplinary planning for new patients." He continued to explain, "Everybody puts their heads together and usually when you present a patient you can tell pretty well what the recommendations are going to be, but occasionally there are little wrinkles you don't think of and sometimes recognizing these wrinkles makes a big difference." He then gave an example of an event in which easily overlooked indicators or, "little wrinkles" were discovered. He explained, "A patient who we saw a few days ago had previously been treated for breast cancer and we had a very experienced breast surgeon who was able to explain why things went wrong (previously) based on his review of the scars from her previous breast surgery."

This particular example illustrates how multi-disciplinary planning for new patients serves to individualize each patient's treatment. The care given to the woman my oncologist was referring to, was individualized. Her physicians at M.D. Anderson "put their heads together" in a successful effort to recognize and explain "little wrinkles" or indicators of failed treatment she had received in the past, so they could understand what may be going wrong in the present and prevent further problems.

When I arrived at M.D. Anderson in April of 2000, my oncologist made me aware of certain treatment plans that probably would have been useless and possibly harmful. I had previously been told that surgery was required. If I had not sought multiple opinions, I would never have known that in my case, surgery prior to chemotherapy, would have been more harmful than beneficial. Persistence saved me from making this huge mistake.

There were two reasons that I needed to be treated with chemotherapy before undergoing surgery. First, the tumor in my left breast had to be shrunk before it could safely be removed. Second, preoperative chemotherapy was needed to kill a majority of the cancer cells that existed throughout my lymphatic system and in my liver. The size of the lump in the breast can indicate the severity of breast cancer and sometimes help to "stage" the cancer. (My breast tumor was 7cm by 4cm, which is very large, and the extent of disease likely meant that my cancer had spread outside of its original location within the breast). Surgery is typically performed to remove a portion of the body in which cancer originates. Cancer cells that may linger and move beyond their original location, often "retaliate" by metastasizing more rapidly and occupying other vital organs in the body. (For example, my cancer had spread, and I also had two tumors in my liver.) My physicians at M.D. Anderson considered my oversized breast tumor as an indication that cancer cells had most likely spread outside of my breast, and so administered preoperative chemotherapy in hope of killing these straying cells. (Many tests were performed in advance and their suspicions were confirmed — as one might guess, the day I learned this, was one of the worst days of my life.) My physicians provided logical reasons for each recommended action. More importantly, they personalized my individual treatment and for this, I will be forever grateful. I believe all cancer patients deserve highly individualized treatment as well. Settle for nothing less. Your expectations should be sky high when it is your life that's in jeopardy!

In summary, listen to your body and the signals it sends you. Obtain multiple opinions to ensure early and proper diagnosis. If possible, choose a hospital that specializes in your particular disease. Rely on your intuition and common sense, and be persistent and determined to find the best physician and a Comprehensive Cancer Center that best fits you and your current condition. The physicians and staff in these centers are qualified to develop and administer the best treatment plan for your illness and you deserve nothing less. Maintain your positive thinking throughout this venture and help as many people as you can along the way. You will survive, you will prevail. Believe.

Chapter 3

The Power of Combining All Medicine

"I believe that the remedial options which exist outside of Western medical practice, should not be considered substitutes, but rather complementary attributes of an integrated treatment program."

Throughout this book, I will be promoting certain forms of alternative medicine: acupuncture, reflexology, colonics, Eastern herbal medicine, proper nutrition and therapeutic massage. These were vital components of my treatment program and I personally, do not consider them to be "alternatives". The word "alternative" tends to imply that such remedies are located on the opposite end of the spectrum in comparison to conventional medicine. I believe that the remedial options which exist outside of Western medical practice, should not be considered substitutes, but rather *complementary* attributes of an integrated treatment program.

The purpose of exhausting all treatment options is to seek all that is necessary to your survival, and potentially beneficial in relieving troublesome or painful side effects of certain types of treatment. Choose components which you and your physician believe will be the most effective, and combine them into a personalized treatment program. Then pursue each vigorously, with an effort to recover and attain a state of wellness that demonstrates "no evidence of disease." Viewing Western and Eastern medicine as separate treatment options is an idea which I strongly urge you to reconsider.

If you have been diagnosed with cancer, Western medicine should be chosen first and foremost, before exploring complementary medicine. Keep in mind that like it or not, health care in the U.S. is big business. Most general physicians are well trained and truly want to do their best for their patients. However, in my experience, unless they are entirely convinced that they are unqualified to treat cancer patients, most doctors are unlikely to refer such patients to a comprehensive cancer center.

Once you have decided on a team that will administer your conventional treatment, you will have reached a point where you can extend your treatment program and supplement Western medicine by incorporating complementary methods. If you can think of your total treatment plan as music, then complementary modalities are but a few notes that are played in order to achieve harmony — they are neither inferior nor superior to Western medicine.

Complementary medicine does not deplore the deficiencies of conventional medicine; instead it intensifies the process of finding a cure and strengthens the effort to heal. In the same respect, my success implies that Western medicine alone does not reign above all other medical practices. The fact that I combined other modalities with my conventional treatment and have thus far survived the most advanced stage of cancer, is what has fueled my belief that Western medicine can successfully incorporate complementary medicine.

According to the mortality statistics relating to Stage IV cancer, I was expected to live for eighteen months (on average), beginning at the point of diagnosis; my chance of survival was three percent or less. Essentially what this means is that historically, Western medicinal practice and its demonstrated capabilities have not proven effective in curing such an advanced stage of illness. It has been over five years, I am still alive with no evidence of disease and my doctors cannot explain why, except for the occasional statement, "you have been very lucky."

It seems odd to me that a physician who specializes in the medical profession, an occupation that requires a great deal of precise science, would refer to a result as "luck." I am not aware of any "luck theory" that exists among scientific discovery or hypothesis. Science is a word that we use to label the pursuit of discovering the undiscovered, explaining the unexplained, and proving what has not yet been proven. In my opinion, "luck" is a word that is used to label events and occurrences that science should be able to explain but unfortunately cannot. Conventional medicine was an important and primary portion of my treatment, yet the doctors who administered my treatment cannot clarify the reason I have been able to triumph over cancer. Obviously, within the realm of Western medicine and the scientific notions that apply, a certain amount of luck was involved in my survival which basically equates to the uncertainty of why I am still alive and in what currently appears to be a disease-free state.

This confusion among my doctors is not a result of incompetence or inexperience. On the contrary, I believe that the doctors I chose were extraordinarily qualified and through my survival, their expertise undoubtedly precedes them. They have mastered the art of Western medicine. However, it is my belief that the abundant education that they acquired within this practice has ironically, reduced their ability to understand and explain my recovery. In order to specialize in the field of cancer all of their focus had to be directed upon the teachings of Western medicine. They were not required to educate themselves about the benefits of complementary modalities. Their understanding is limited in regard to the treatment I pursued outside of the conventional boundaries in which they practice. When they ponder the reason for my survival they only think in terms of what they know and have studied and do not consider factors (such as complementary medicine) of which their knowledge is limited or impartial. Therefore, when I heard my doctors refer to "luck", in my mind it translated as a lack of understanding the potential benefits of integrating complementary medicine in order to strengthen or broaden the reach of Western medicine.

There are three main procedures that are used in Western medicine to combat cancer: surgery, radiation and chemotherapy. In a surgical operation, a tumor or section of the body where tumors are located is removed. Chemotherapy is the use of cytotoxic chemicals meant to kill cancer cells. According to Col. Shriver, "In some patients it would appear that chemotherapy kills, if not all breast cancer cells (that are out there somewhere waiting to continue to grow in the future), it kills enough of them so that the body's immune system can take over and kill the rest of the cells."

One benefits from chemotherapy's ability to destroy cancer cells, but it may not kill all cancer cells present and in its attempt to do so it will also kill good white blood cells or T-cells. White blood cells are your body's natural defense against disease. Therefore, chemo drastically decreases the effectiveness of your immune system. On this topic, Col. Shriver states "We definitely know that the immune system plays a role in keeping cancers in check or preventing them from spreading… it's a very complex interplay between the cancer, the body's immune system, the person, the genetics, the environment, the diet."

Having a strong immune system is important and complementary medicine places significant emphasis on strengthening the immune system. While chemo kills the cancer cells, complementary modalities can be employed to reinforce the body's natural immunity, providing the body the ability to attack disease (thereby complementing chemo's ability to kill cancer cells).

Col. Shriver openly expresses the great importance of the body's immune system in the survival of cancer: "…the truth of the matter is, we don't know in an individual patient whether it [chemotherapy] is going to work — to kill all or enough of the cancer cells, so that the immune system can take over and do the rest of the job and prevent cancer from coming back in the future." I interpret his statement basically to mean that the immune system needs to be strong if you are going to survive long-term. Complementary medicine can be incorporated into your overall treatment, specifically for this purpose.

Proper nutrition, acupuncture, therapeutic massage, reflexology, and colonics, are all complementary modalities which I believe dramatically strengthened my immune system, either directly or indirectly. I know that these remedies, combined with my conventional treatment worked hand in hand, to contribute to my survival. I feel that if you believe and are committed to your treatment plan, you too, can achieve the same result.

Chapter 4

The Power of Acupuncture

"It is time to ambush and surround your illness by employing every possible modality that can potentially attack cancer cells."

Acupuncture is a word that many people recognize but are often uncertain as to what it really is. This form of therapy is growing rapidly in popularity in the United States. However, it has not been a commonly accepted form of treatment in our cultural history. The majority of our country's medical practices consist of Western medicine, although the benefits of complementary Eastern remedies are becoming more widely understood, bolstered by the testimony of those who have experienced their healing power.

Every year there is more empirical evidence to support the effectiveness of acupuncture. I believe it successfully supplemented my conventional treatment in such a way that leads me to stress the importance of its consideration and possible trial.

As discussed previously, treatment is often more successful when highly individualized, and it is possible that acupuncture may not be the best option for you. That being said, I ask you to keep an open mind, realize that you could possibly benefit from acupuncture, and avoid the tendency to rely solely upon Western treatment regimes. It is time to ambush and surround your illness by employing every possible modality that can potentially attack cancer cells. There is no doubt that our culture has made fantastic strides in health care in general, and much has been learned about cancer and how to combat it in the past fifty years. However, I believe that to view our Western treatments as superior, or as your only option, is off base. As you know, there is a vast world that exists beyond the United States, and there are various treatments that have existed in some cases, for thousands of years, in cultures that extend far beyond our own country's borders. Please do not dismiss these treatments simply because they seem strange or unfamiliar. Acupuncture could indeed prove to be a valuable ally in your fight against cancer.

In reality, many forms of conventional treatment rely on concepts that are similar to the ideology that acupuncture is based upon. Some of the most technological and scientific Western modalities are administered according to, and based on the flow of energy that exists in our bodies. Acupuncture seeks to manipulate these currents of energy so as to relieve pain, stress, inflammation, nausea, fatigue, etc. The usefulness of acupuncture as it relates to cancer is that among other benefits, it can greatly reduce the side effects of chemotherapy. The very ailments that acupuncture can alleviate are coincidentally, some of the drawbacks of conventional treatment.

I promote the complementary use of acupuncture because it has proven to be beneficial throughout the duration of my cancer journey. However, I will not go as far as to say that acupuncture should be seriously considered by every cancer patient, as it simply may not be suitable for everyone. However, I have written this book with the intention of helping anyone with cancer and so, if acupuncture assists only one reader, then I will have achieved my goal. You may be that person. I challenge you to consider this option. There is of course, no guarantee that acupuncture will work for you and meet your approval. I only know that it is worthy of my praise, and that many others have experienced its effectiveness. It merits consideration and experimentation since it offers possible relief of painful and troublesome side effects. A dear friend, Marilyn, incorporated acupuncture as part of her treatment plan. Marilyn was able to play tennis up until one month prior to her death. I believe that acupuncture can help improve the quality of life for some cancer patients, and that, to me, is invaluable.

What is Acupuncture? Yes, acupuncture involves the insertion of needles into the skin. However, if one can look beyond that physical act, one will see that acupuncture is far more. Acupuncture has often been misunderstood. It is a medical practice that has been studied for centuries and mastered by Chinese and Japanese medicine men and women known as Shamans. The treatment can be traced back to ancient China, with the first records implying its use, being dated to 1600 B.C. It has survived the centuries and continually progressed to its current form. There is a very good reason that it has been around for so long and continues to be used. Through the ages, acupuncture has been proven to be an effective and therefore, valued form of healing.

While acupuncture is not necessarily included in the protocol of Western medicine, its use was approved by the Federal Drug Administration (FDA) in the early 1990s. The FDA recognized it to be beneficial in relieving pain and nausea especially among cancer patients receiving chemotherapy. This alone demonstrates that Western medicine practitioners in the United States are becoming increasingly aware of and comfortable with what acupuncture has to offer.

Understanding how and why acupuncture works will allow you to make a sound decision as to whether or not it may be of value as part of your total treatment plan. While I am not a qualified professional in the practice of acupuncture, I have researched its basic concepts and directly experienced its benefits. I found that besides strengthening my immune system to help combat cancer cells, it also greatly reduced the side effects of my chemotherapy. You don't have to be an expert to understand the basic concepts of acupuncture.

The main concept of acupuncture involves the manipulation of energy, that is, the flow of energy that is constantly pulsing throughout our bodies. These currents flow up and down pathways that are known as meridians, which are located on each side of the body and extend vertically from head to toe, and limb to limb. There are a total of twenty meridians, twelve being principal and eight that are secondary. Each meridian is unique and is associated with a certain organ such as the liver, heart, lung, intestine, or with an organ system such as the nervous, respiratory, digestive, or excretory system, etc. Meridians are the channels that carry our inner life force.

This notion of a "map" of meridians, is quite possibly a new concept to you. If you are doubtful or disbelieving, then consider the basics of science and biology. We are well aware that everything tangible on this earth contains energy. Whether it is a human being or a pencil you write with, all matter contains a certain degree of energy. The human body binds an enormous energy flow. With the invention of the atomic bomb, Einstein proved how powerful the energy within our bodies can be. By splitting a simple atom, Einstein was able to create an overload of energy powerful enough to destroy a large geographic area. Every cell in our bodies contains atoms which are composed of protons, neutrons, and electrons. This is energy in its smallest form. The main component of what can be the most powerful manifestation of energy, can be found in your body, in each and every one of your cells.

Our main source of energy exists in our brain and nervous system. The brain encodes and decodes messages that are transported by our neuron cells to the part of the body that will carry out the particular function that each message transmits. Our neuron cells extend throughout our entire body and the impulses that they carry are electronic, which produces the constant flow of energy that travels through our body. Acupuncture uses this energy to heal and strengthen.

Consider this: a person is not entirely dead if his/her heart stops beating. Death is clinically pronounced when brain activity ceases — when the source of the energy flow is no longer functioning or producing energy. Your heart beat can be revived, and this is often accomplished by administering an electrical shock that basically jumpstarts your heart and does so through the use of energy.

The nutrients in the food we consume are used for energy to power the body. Both the brain and nervous system use this energy to transmit the involuntary and voluntary functions of the rest of the body. Involuntary refers to the functions of your organ systems and voluntary functions generally consist of the movements and actions that you make of which you are immediately aware. These functions result in the depletion of energy which leads to the need for replenishment. The overall result, is that our bodies feed off energy, produce more energy, and release energy in a repetitive and continual process in order to survive. Anything that facilitates or strengthens this process, greatly contributes to one's overall wellness.

Acupuncture strives to increase as well as suppress, or sedate energy, in order to create a balance in its flow. Certain currents of energy in the human body, will go "haywire" or be weakened, usually as a result of external factors such as stress. Acupuncture is a process that either tranquilizes energy that is out of control, or stimulates the flow of energy that has become exhausted. This is done by the insertion of thin needles into acupoints located along the meridians described earlier. There are over a thousand points of insertion. Each point exists as either a strengthening or sedating point. The needles are inserted millimeters beneath the skin and serve to either interfere with the flow of energy in order to slow its overflow, or stimulate the current of energy to increase its volume. Once again, meridians are the paths of energy that relate to various parts of the body that energy is flowing to, and acupoints indicate where each needle should be placed in accordance with each meridian.

An excess of energy or lack thereof can dramatically increase stress, both mentally and physically. Stress is a factor that can have a very significant and negative impact on one's mental attitude, immune system, and overall wellness. It has been proven that stress is a main cause of illness and I believe that it had a direct effect on the origins of my cancer. Stress seems to feed upon the pain and suffering it causes and in doing so, becomes stronger, more intense and increasingly difficult to bear.

Chemotherapy produces side effects that typically increase stress. Fatigue, nausea, and pain are dangerous stressors that decrease one's overall wellness. Acupuncture can relieve these ailments and in doing so, it will reduce stress which in turn, strengthens your immune system and empowers it to better fight cancer cells. While chemotherapy may kill cancer cells, at the same time it is poisoning your body and inhibiting the natural abilities of the immune system to combat cancer. Therefore, if acupuncture can strengthen the immune system, it can serve as a beneficial complement to conventional medicine. I encourage you to research and experiment with acupuncture so that you can make an informed decision as to whether it is an appropriate complementary treatment for you.

Should you choose to try acupuncture, approach it in a manner similar to that described in the earlier chapter about seeking multiple opinions. Investigate the credentials of the acupuncturist to ensure that he/she is qualified to administer the treatment. If not, then move on to another practitioner or ask a member of your treatment team for a recommendation. I found a qualified individual through a referral from my nutritionist. And of course, bedside manner is very important. Be certain you trust and feel comfortable with every member of your "wellness team".

Discuss the manner in which treatment is administered, so you will know exactly what to expect. Chances are this is a new procedure for you, so you'll want your practitioner to be forthcoming with a description of the process. As with any clinical procedure, sterility is of the utmost importance. All of the needles should be sterile and disposable. When you receive a vaccination, the area to be injected is sterilized (usually with alcohol); your acupuncturist should do the same.

Inquire as to the short and long-term cost involved, as it will depend on the frequency and duration of the treatments. Prior to agreeing to treatment, consult your insurance company in order to learn the extent of coverage they will provide for you, if any.

Do not be afraid of offending the practitioner by asking these questions. This form of treatment is highly personalized and focused on the comfort of the patient. Your inquiries will most likely be welcomed. You in turn, will be asked numerous questions on your first appointment, in an effort to gather medical information about you as an individual and as a patient, so that the treatment can be conducted most effectively. The flow of energy is affected by wellness, lifestyle, and behavioral patterns and these are naturally different for each person. Therefore, each patient's acupuncture treatment will vary according to his/her unique condition and state of wellness.

My own instincts compelled me to research other modalities in order to achieve overall success in my fight against cancer. If I had not incorporated complements such as acupuncture, I do not believe I would be alive and in good health today. While conventional treatment contributed a great deal to my recovery, it was interesting to witness my physicians' astonishment, confusion, and inability to understand or explain how I was improving so rapidly. My conventional physicians (i.e., practicing Western medicine) eventually realized how beneficial it was to integrate other forms of medicine into my treatment plan.

In my opinion, complementary medicine is essential to your treatment. An integrated approach can bring you closer to perfection in terms of your treatment, and acupuncture can be a valuable part of your overall plan. Remember to use this treatment time to incorporate visualization into your wellness program — picture yourself whole and well, progressing along the triumphant path of your cancer journey. Imagine that the acupuncture needles are arrows penetrating cancer cells in your body, and visualize those evil cells being destroyed! Strive to strengthen your immune system and achieve overall wellness. If acupuncture proves to be beneficial to you and if you believe in its effectiveness, then you will be one step closer to your long-term, disease-free survival.

"Life is not about
significant details, illuminated
in a flash, fixed forever.
Photographs are."
--- Susan Sontag

My husband John and I, Summer, 1995! Our first summer
together! One of my favorite photos "pre-cancer". Life was great!

Summer, 1999 on vacation in Colorado with John and my son Colby!
I thought life was amazing then, but now I appreciate it even more!

Two days after my Stage IV cancer diagnosis in Houston, Texas. I was scheduled to have a catheter inserted and begin a clinical trial the next morning at M.D. Anderson Cancer Center. It was all we could do to force a smile.

John's sons, Danny and Anthony with Colby (in the center); Summer, 2000 — so much to live for!

Labor Day weekend, 2000; three weeks prior to the experimental radio-frequency ablation at MDACC.

Christmas, 2000 – Smiles that Christmas were few and far between. We still did not know what to expect.

New Year's, 2001 – at The Hibachi on The Country Club Plaza
in Kansas City, Missouri. My favorite place to eat! We always
seem to meet our friends there! (Boy, was that wig bad!)

Spring, 2001 – searching my soul for strength at the
height of my chemotherapy treatments.

I prayed to my angels every day many, many times.

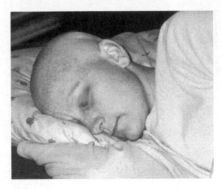

Sleep . . . my only escape from the pain of mouth sores and all the other side effects of intense chemotherapy for nearly a year.

John & I renewing our wedding vows September, 2001. My hair was
starting to grow back! We shared the special day with our closest friends!
I was beginning to feel more optimistic about the path I was on.

October, 2001 — my first visit with Dr. Yeshi Dhonden in Berkeley, California. I continue to see him every six months during his U.S. visits! He gives me strength and courage to fight for my life.

Summer, 2002 – John's dream trip of a lifetime to Zimbabwe! I was feeling better for the first time since April, 2000. I began this book while he and Colby hunted the Plains game!

My namesake, Capri Jo Thoman. Yet another reason to live!

October, 2002 — Lara Moritz & me! Our friendship had just begun!

October, 2002 — Katie Harman, Miss America 2002, her mother,
Darla Harman, my mom, Linda Wittmeyer and me! Having
Katie convey our Foundation's message of hope and awareness
across the nation has been one of my dreams come true!

October, 2002 — with my Dad, Larry Wittmeyer, and my
step-mom, Sheila, at the Lori C. Lober Cancer Foundation
first annual black tie gala, held at the Building for a Cure
Designer Show Home, Kansas City, Missouri.

Summer 2003 – John and I after a lot of hard days. Although I continued
to worry about the cancer returning, happier days had arrived!

June, 2003 — Colonel and Mrs. Craig Shriver. We met them at the
wedding of Katie Harman and Tim Ebner in Portland, Oregon.

**Summer 2003 – With my sweet Colby at Moon Palace in Cancun,
Mexico! I love any time we get to spend together! The fresh
air and sunshine was very therapeutic and healing for me!**

My surprise 40th birthday party! Who said I would never see 40?
A girl can never have too many friends! I have been blessed!

Christmas, 2003 — on a trip to Las Vegas with friends Lori and Ted Maguire and Jami and John Hepting (who's taking the photo). Life is great! I wouldn't trade the journey I've been on for anything in the world.

2003 —with our great friends, Kendra and Bob Wooldridge and Laura and Bob Myer, Kansas City Builders Club trip to Grand Cayman Island.

New York City, Spring, 2004 — with fellow Kansas Citian and breast cancer survivor, Kim Carlos. Kim and I were two of twenty-five individuals chosen nationwide as Yoplait Champions in the fight against breast cancer, sponsored by Yoplait, the Susan G. Komen Breast Cancer Foundation and SELF Magazine.

Paris, July 2004 — with Jami and John Hepting (center) and
some fellow Americans on the Champs Elysee, cheering on my
hero and inspiration, Lance Armstrong at the Tour de France.

Fall, 2004 — With my Dad, Larry Wittmeyer and brother, Larry, Jr.

John has carried me through the hard times! I
really think I'm going to be ok now!

Chapter 5

The Power of Proper Nutrition

"We have made great progress in understanding cancer. The cause of breast cancer, as an example, is usually multi-factorial. It involves gene mutations as well as various environmental exposures and lifestyle choices. It is very complex in every patient and so the cure of breast cancer will very much depend on patients changing their habits. Why do Western women have more breast cancer than Eastern/Asian women? The answer seems to be in the diet. That is a choice... processed foods, foods that are high in things that lead to increased estrogen levels in women, increased obesity which also increases the risk of breast cancer because it increases circulating estrogen levels... these are lifestyle choices."

Col. Craig Shriver, M.D., F.A.C.S., M.C.

"You are what you eat..." I'm sure you've heard this phrase once if not a thousand times, along with other sayings such as, "eat to live, don't live to eat" or "your body is a temple." For some, especially those who are healthy, these phrases may seem trite, but they hold significant meaning: what we put into our bodies, has a direct effect on how much energy we can produce.

Proper nutrition and supplementation is vital to your health. When you are fighting cancer, your survival depends upon your overall wellness, which in turn is driven in large part by nutrition. Question your physician if he/she tells you, "Go ahead and eat what you want, enjoy your life while you still can." At the time I was diagnosed with Stage IV cancer, one of my many physicians said this to me. I am very grateful that I chose not to take this advice. I wasn't about to bow down to cancer by thinking, "I am going to enjoy my life until my illness takes it from me." Instead, I planned to defeat cancer by empowering my mind and body to fight it. Simple common sense and logic helped me to realize that an enormous component of "living well" is "eating well."

When you are diagnosed with cancer, it's so easy to "comfort" yourself with foods that seem to "feed" emotional needs. For example, we're all familiar with how some people develop cravings for chocolate, something akin to an emotional attachment. Chocolate is even thought of as an "aphrodisiac." I'm sure you have heard someone say, "I have a bit of a sweet tooth." A person may be a chocolate lover or enjoy dessert after each meal, but this is not due to heredity or genetics. A "sweet tooth" is nothing more than an attachment to sweet foods that develops as a result of consistently eating foods that are high in sugar. But cancer patients beware — cancer is fueled by eating sugar and foods that turn to sugar when consumed – NO MORE SUGAR.

Upon gaining extra weight, many people go on fad diets, and even fast. In many cases, people have success with these methods and drop the excess weight. Unfortunately, a majority eventually gain back the pounds. If you are among this group, and you plot the fluctuation of your weight on a timeline, you may find that your body weight has been rising and falling sporadically. This inconsistency will not help you to achieve the balance and tranquility needed for optimal wellness. Cancer causes disorder and chaos within your body. In order to survive, you must restore your body's equilibrium.

A large portion of balancing nutrition lies in maintaining a healthy, natural body weight. Obviously, some people naturally have a larger percentage of body fat than others. If you believe you are overweight, don't focus on shedding pounds. If you see yourself as overly thin, don't concentrate on gaining weight. Instead, if you direct your effort solely at proper nutrition, your body weight will gradually approach a natural, healthy level for you. In practicing proper nutrition, you are not dieting, you are not fasting, and you are not overeating; rather, you are simply consuming and absorbing the appropriate vitamins, minerals and nutrients your body needs in order to function at its peak.

My cancer diagnosis forced me to change my lifestyle. Eating well is a matter of knowing exactly what it is you are consuming and how it affects your bodily functions and overall health. It requires knowing how and when you should eat certain foods and drink certain liquids.

It may be helpful to consult with a holistic nutritionist who can, if appropriate, prescribe all-natural vitamin and mineral supplements that are beneficial to the immune system. The human body's immune system is an intricate network of specialized tissues, organs, cells and chemicals. The lymph nodes, spleen, bone marrow, thymus gland, and tonsils all play a role in fighting off germs and illnesses. When the immune system is functioning well, it is able to neutralize potentially infectious organisms before an infection can develop. The immune system also looks for cells in the body that could "morph" into cancerous cells and attempts to eradicate them.

Although diet and lifestyle both play a crucial role in maintaining a healthy immune system, equally important are immune-regulating herbs and supplements. Of course, many can benefit from immune-balancing herbs and supplements, but those with cancer or other illnesses or allergies, are likely to benefit most.

I talked with cancer survivors and took my nutritionist's advice. Together, we developed a nutritional plan designed to help combat cancer. Before my diagnosis, I made an effort to stay healthy by attempting to include the five food groups in each meal. As a cancer patient, I now realize that generally, much of what we've been taught about nutrition is not entirely accurate.

The body absorbs the vitamins, minerals and nutrients that it needs and passes on whatever is left as waste. This complex process requires energy. Different foods require the digestive system to use diverse amounts of energy. Protein, for example, takes more time and energy to digest than carbohydrates, while fruits take the least amount of time and energy. Your body can digest and put to use only two types of food at one time. You can benefit from a protein and a starch, but if you add a vegetable then one of the food groups will go to waste. In other words, in my opinion, there is little, if any advantage to combining all five food groups at one meal. By eating five food groups in one sitting, basically, you are consuming more food than the body can handle. Only a portion of that food is actually used beneficially, the rest is stored as fat, passed through as waste, or collected as putrefaction along the walls of the colon. Instead of attempting to fit all five food groups into three full meals a day, focus on eating two food groups within five balanced, smaller meals, at least two hours apart, each day.

In the morning, I focus solely on eating foods that will alkaline my body. According to my nutritionist, an "alkalined body" is one nurtured with fruit and reverse-osmosis water (ultra-refined water). While drinking water should be continual throughout each day, fruit is most beneficial when consumed before noon. Fruit is digested faster than carbohydrates or proteins and should not be combined with any other food group. I would not recommend that fruit be mixed with any substance other than water. If the body is digesting a protein and fruit is consumed, the fruit will be passed quickly with little benefit. The protein is fully absorbed but the fruit goes to waste.

Combine portions of fruit with a few glasses of *purified* water. Do not drink tap water. If you do not have a water purifier then if possible, have one installed. Another option would be bottled water but you must be careful which brand you choose to purchase. My nutritionist recommended that I drink what she described as *reverse osmosis* water. Whether you choose to install a purifier or purchase bottled water, make certain that you are consuming water that's as untainted and as decontaminated as possible.

It is recommended that a person drink at least eight glasses of water a day, however, as many as ten to twelve glasses can't hurt. At the height of my chemo treatments I was trying to drink twenty glasses of water a day. What's important is that you continue to make a conscious effort to hydrate your body each day. Don't be concerned with drinking too much water. There is no such thing as drinking too much, given that water is the only substance that is safely consumed in excess.

Water should be your number one source of liquid, the second being green, red or white tea. If you drink any fruit juice, I recommend that it be freshly squeezed or blended instead of bought by the container. At the grocery store, the foods and liquids sold in cans, jugs, bottles etc. are generally processed and filled with unnatural preservatives. Besides, when is the last time you have enjoyed freshly squeezed orange juice?

In the afternoon and evening you can focus on consuming proteins, vegetables and carbohydrates. The sources I would recommend for protein would be: beans, seeds and raw, unsalted nuts. Meat cooked by gas and charcoal contains carcinogens which basically can cause or fuel cancer cells.

Eat raw or lightly steamed vegetables that provide your body with an abundance of nutrients. Raw or steamed broccoli, carrots, corn, asparagus or peas, would be great choices for afternoon or evening meals. Eat a steamed vegetable along with a protein and you have yourself a perfectly healthy and "properly combined" meal.

You can alternate carbohydrates and proteins in such a meal but I recommend that you always have vegetables with your afternoon and evening meals. If you choose to have carbohydrates with your vegetables, remember that any white bread, white pasta, or white rice will be processed into sugar (which fuels cancer). Whole wheat or whole grain bread and pasta is a better choice.

Proper diet and keeping stress under control will enable your body to better fight cancer—and that's what it's all about!!!

Note: I personally have found taking Noxylane, or AHCC (Alpha Hexose Correlated Compound), high-powered mushroom supplements, to be very beneficial. I have now been taking them for over five years and in spite of all the chemo I have endured, I feel these have helped keep my immune system strong. By encouraging the development of large numbers of highly active granules within the NK (natural killer) cells, mushroom compounds work to "tune up" the immune system while optimizing T, B, and NK cell function. Published studies have shown mushrooms to increase NK cell activity by more than 300%, B cell activity by 250% or greater, and T cell activity by 200% --- better than other vitamin, herbal or medicinal mushroom therapies. For more information regarding these supplements, log onto www.lanelabs.com or www.ahccpublishedresearch.com.

Chapter 6

The Power of Colonics

"An unhealthy colon is toxic to the body and cancer feeds off impurities. You can either allow your colon to be a means for cancer to become stronger and possibly metastasize, or you can empower the colon to produce an environment that is in effect "too healthy and efficient" for cancer to prevail."

As you may guess, colonics has to do with the colon. The small intestine and the colon – the large intestine – are the body's vessels for transporting bodily waste from the stomach to the rectum. There are other organs and glands that assist in this process and they are directly impacted by the condition of the colon; but make no mistake about it, the colon can affect every aspect of the body, either directly or indirectly. The majority of our organs have more than one function, so what affects a given organ, will likely affect those that work in concert with it, (one reason why cancer can spread so rapidly from one organ to the next). An unhealthy colon is toxic to the body and cancer feeds off impurities. You can either allow your colon to be a means for cancer to become stronger and possibly metastasize, or you can empower the colon to produce an environment that is in effect "too healthy and efficient" for cancer to prevail.

While cancer may thrive on our weaknesses, the body feeds off its own strengths. By strengthening the colon you can also improve the kidneys, the liver, the heart, the mind, the immune system, and so on.

Under normal circumstances the body is well equipped to neutralize and dispose of toxins through the liver, spleen, and other eliminative channels. However, as a Stage IV cancer patient, my circumstances were far from "normal". I felt I needed to do more to augment my conventional medicine treatment plan, to help increase my chances of survival.

Colonics is another complement I chose to employ, that I feel positively impacted the results of my conventional treatment. While certainly not obvious, the colon needs to be cared for in order to achieve wellness. The colon affects the overall functions of the body and so its empowerment is essential. The food that you eat is processed through the body in a way that aims to make use of all nutrients to produce energy that is needed in order for the body to function properly. These nutrients are transported throughout the entire body, from glands to organs, from organs to organ systems. The colon is one of the main processes of this transportation. If it is not functioning properly, the body and all of its components will not receive the proper level of nutrients needed.

The colon transfers waste from the food we eat to the rectum where it is expelled from the body. As a result of improper nutrition, the colon becomes clogged with putrefied waste which disrupts the process of elimination and leads to more putrefaction. Maintaining proper digestive and eliminative functions entails having two to three bowel movements per day on a regular basis. Most people are not aware of this. Infants offer a good illustration: ask any mother – a baby will eat and almost immediately eliminate. Their new digestive systems have not had time to develop the mal-absorption problems caused by improper diet, environmental toxins and stress. Faulty digestion and elimination develop in an individual through years of improper lifestyle and dietary habits.

Proper Nutrition. There is much that you can do to improve the condition and functioning of your colon by eating the proper foods. Proper nutrition is lacking in our society. The overall diet of the population in the United States consists mainly of high sodium, sugar, red meat, and processed foods that contribute to the putrefaction that occurs in the colon. Much of the fatty acids and toxic chemicals that are in red meats and processed foods for example, are collected along the walls of the colon in putrefied fecal matter. While the body does manage to absorb what nutrients it can from these foods, they produce a greater proportion of matter that is unnecessary and even harmful. These foods do not help to cleanse, but rather, their by-products collect and become toxic to the body. The overall result is an over-abundance of waste and a lack of nutrition.

Before I was diagnosed with cancer, like most Americans, I enjoyed fast foods like buffalo chicken wings, cheeseburgers, etc. Having a fresh, green salad every now and then was definitely not enough. My cancer diagnosis required that I eat foods that could strengthen my body, help fight the cancer and increase my chance of survival. I needed foods that contained an abundance of nutrients that my body could use to empower itself. The nutrient that best serves the colon is fiber.

Fiber exists in foods such as beans, seeds, raw fruits, and vegetables. These foods also contain the vitamins and minerals that the body needs to function at its best without producing a large amount of excess waste. Many people refer to fruits and vegetables as roughage and this interpretation is accurate in that their rough texture often serves to sweep through the colon, collecting some of the putrefied waste that exists along its walls. When you eat such foods and your bowel movements seem to increase, it is not because more waste has been produced, but because in addition to a normal amount of waste, these fiber-rich foods are carrying along what had already existed and putrefied in the colon.

Colon Irrigation. As discussed earlier, putrefaction is basically the collection of waste around the inner walls of the colon, which directly interferes with the absorption of nutrients and the elimination of needless waste. In my opinion, the best way to keep this from occurring is the process of colon irrigation. While these two words may conjure some unpleasant thoughts, I anticipate that this chapter will convey the message that colon irrigations are not unpleasant. In fact, in my opinion, the benefits of colonics, including colon irrigation, will produce comforting results that will prove to be effective. I actually feel very good following a colon therapy session.

Eating the right foods is only part of what is needed to ensure a healthy colon. While it may seem that proper nutrition is a reasonable solution, in my opinion, colon irrigations are still a necessity. Chances are that you have not eaten properly on a consistent basis throughout your life and quite possibly for your entire life. This being so, the amount of putrefaction that has continually accumulated up to now, must be taken into account.

The consumption of proper foods can only cleanse your colon in the length of time it takes for them to pass through your system. Your colon may require greater focus and care to achieve a thorough cleansing (especially if you are over thirty). In many cases, the colon becomes so clogged that even the most beneficial foods cannot entirely pass through the colon and they collect and then putrefy along its walls. In this event, your body actually becomes unable to absorb all of the nutrients you consume. This alone, greatly weakens your body's ability to function properly and can be very detrimental to your health and wellness. Fortunately, colonics is a worthwhile solution to this problem.

In the book entitled "Colon Health: The Key to a Vibrant Life", Dr. Norman W. Walker states, "one should receive at least six colon irrigations every year" in order to ensure a healthy colon. While you should receive a number of irrigations annually, do not be deterred, for it is not an exhausting process. Unlike some chemotherapy, colon irrigations are not grueling, painful treatments. Irrigations cleanse and massage the interior of the colon by releasing small increments of water into the colon throughout a time period of thirty to forty-five minutes. While it may be awkward to have another individual perform this treatment on you, it is not painful (just remind yourself why you are having it done). You will gradually become more comfortable with the process once you experience the positive results that follow. What can be accomplished in a relatively short time period is well worth the effort it takes to find a qualified colonics practitioner (a Certified Colon Therapist) and receive the treatment. In doing so, your body will become able to absorb all nutrients and process all waste without complications. This will energize your body and allow it to fight your illness by surrounding and attacking the plaguing invasion on a healthy front.

Colon irrigations also increase wellness by detoxifying the body. Red meats and processed foods contain toxins that collect and putrefy in the colon. Once consumed, these toxins are released into the body. Once they accumulate in putrefied waste, their toxicity increases. If you leave a glass of water out on a table for a few days, it will become contaminated. If the water was impure when it was first poured, then its quality will be even more unsanitary. While water does not contain its own filtration system, fortunately, our bodies do. Even so, eventual maintenance is required given that this system was not meant to prevail over an imbalance of abundant waste and limited nutrients (there is only so much we can expect of our bodies!).

Over time, the developed mass of rancid waste ferments and the colon becomes increasingly more polluted. As your body continues to carry out its filtration process, some of the toxins that have fermented in your colon are absorbed in the mix of incoming nutrients and passed through your blood to other organs and organ systems. This is why you must continually guard against putrefaction and fermentation.

A synonym of the word 'ferment' is 'turmoil', which is exactly what cancer creates within your body. An antonym for turmoil is order, such as the organized functioning of a clean and healthy colon. This can be achieved through colon irrigations and proper nutrition. In other words, order is the solution to chaos and one of the keys to eliminating cancer. If you truly want to survive, you must seek out all treatment options that create stability, evaluate the feasibility of each for your own unique situation, and seize those opportunities which offer the greatest promise. Colonics is an option that I believe put me in a much stronger position to fight off cancer.

We have discussed how colonics allows your body to properly absorb nutrients, and how it detoxifies your body by preventing the fermentation of putrefied waste. However, there is yet another potential benefit colonics can provide.

Putrefaction causes abnormal inflammation or swelling of the colon which could have a harmful effect on organs that are located near the colon. Physical pressure is inflicted upon organs that are in close proximity to an inflamed colon. Those who have cancer of the bladder or the prostate are particularly susceptible to such pressure. The bladder and the prostate are located near the colon, which if inflamed, applies unnatural force upon them, causing stress that will disrupt their proper functioning. This also impairs the ability of the prostate and the bladder to assist the functioning of other related organs.

Inflammation of the colon can also affect the liver, kidneys, pancreas, spleen, reproductive organs, diaphragm, and stomach. These organs are all located near the colon.

Civilization has progressed because of our ability to interact and learn from each other. It seems fitting that the systemic functions of our bodies thrive from the same interactive cooperation. First, we must learn and better ourselves before we can change the world around us. In converting your illness into wellness, you must learn to strengthen your mind and body so that its systems interact with each other in a way which promotes the proper functioning of a healthy, fit body. You must continue to have a positive and active attitude. Seek out a certified colon therapist in your area and see for yourself how cleansed you feel afterward.

The choices you make and the actions you take will dictate the wellness of your body. Choosing colonics could be a big step forward in your road to recovery. I challenge you to seriously consider this option and its many benefits. You can cleanse your body of toxins and prevent the harm they cause. Your body will absorb nutrients and produce an abundance of energy that is ever-flowing in the right direction. Remember, you want to be constantly moving forward toward your long-term survival. I believe colonics is a key factor that will greatly assist you in doing so. The power that you have is limitless. Use it and you will prevail.

Chapter 7

The Power of Body Work

"Massage doesn't just feel good. Research shows it reduces the heart rate, increases the blood circulation and lymph flow, relaxes muscles, improves range of motion, increases endorphins (the body's natural pain killers) and more."

It was May 1, 2000 and I had just received my first chemotherapy treatment at the M.D. Anderson Cancer Center (MDACC) in Houston, Texas. The same evening, we were to attend an awards banquet immediately following our flight to Kansas City from Houston. The banquet was the local Home Builder Association's "American Dream Awards" contest ceremony. My husband John, son Colby and I met our good friends Bob & Laura Myer and Bob & Kendra Wooldridge at the event. I felt like all my home-building industry colleagues, friends and acquaintances looked at me differently that evening – *"Now I am different – I have cancer"* is how I felt. Some offered genuine sympathy, while others seemed afraid of me – as if they were afraid they may "catch cancer" from me. It was a very strange night. Five years later, I still remember telling myself that night, *"This is NOT the end of Lori Lober."* I was convinced that the clinical trial I was participating in at MDACC was a great choice, but in my heart and soul I continued to feel that I needed to do more.

I'm not sure why, but the first thing I did after we returned home from Houston was visit a book store near our home in Kansas City. In reality,

I couldn't wait to research reflexology — another possibly beneficial therapy — to explore any possible contribution it may make to my overall wellness. I had no prior knowledge of reflexology and obviously had never experienced any treatments. What little I knew about it was that each point in the hands and feet is somehow related to specific points in the body. It was time for me to get serious. Once again, I needed to take matters into my own hands and further coordinate my "journey to wellness".

I purchased several books on reflexology that day. I looked at the diagrams and focused on the points representing key areas of my body — my breasts, my liver, etc. Because cancer had spread throughout my lymphatic system, I researched that as well. I immediately began to treat myself. Every now and then, my husband John would do it for me. I visualized all the cancer leaving my body as I would treat myself, sometimes so vigorously that my fingers would hurt from the pressure I was applying. Each day I would give myself these "treatments", sometimes as often as three times a day! It would be a little while however, before I sought professional treatment, as life was about to offer me another unexpected surprise, but this time, a very pleasant one.

A Forever Friend. I had been continuously putting the word out that I was very eager to find another Stage IV breast cancer patient who was doing well. I knew she was out there and if I could find her, she would give me hope!

One day John called me — he had just spoken with one of our new homeowners who had heard of my recent cancer diagnosis. She believed that one of her neighbors had exactly the same type of cancer that I had and she was doing exceptionally well! Without skipping a beat, I picked up the phone and called our client to discuss it with her.

Within a few days, Connie and I talked on the phone. We compared stories. It was so incredibly comforting to speak with someone who understood everything I was feeling. She knew the lingo, she could relate to my fears – she was my angel on earth! I was so happy. She was cute and spunky and she was "beating the odds"! After meeting Connie and witnessing her strength, I never again felt sorry for myself. She inspired me to fight like hell and now I knew that I, too, could really win --- she was proof!

Connie and I would have lunch together and talk about our husbands and our kids. We would talk about proper nutrition and what she was juicing as we chatted on the phone first thing in the morning. We would talk about anything and everything that was currently consuming our lives. We quickly became close friends.

I told Connie of my desire to begin receiving therapeutic massage and professional reflexology. She had a wonderful friend that did therapeutic massage! If Connie believed in her and trusted her, that was enough for me. I first met Vonnie, a retired nurse who has practiced therapeutic massage for 12 years, just two months into my "journey to wellness". Not only did I feel it was important to professionally treat my lymphatic system with massage, but it could help alleviate stress as well. (Living each day with the realization that I may be dying, was and still is *extremely stressful*. While there is currently "no evidence of disease" in my body, the knowledge that the cancer can return, can at times, be stressful and draining. It is key for cancer patients to control and limit stress in their daily lives, as cancer cells can "feed" off stress). In addition, the side effects of two rounds of chemotherapy were beginning to slow me down.

Therapeutic Massage. Therapeutic massage involves the manipulation of the soft tissue structures of the body. Its goal is to alleviate pain, discomfort, muscle spasms, and stress. The American Massage Therapy Association (AMTA) defines massage therapy as a profession in which the practitioner applies manual pressure with the intention of positively affecting the health and well being of the client. The AMTA works to establish massage therapy as integral to the maintenance of good health and complementary to other therapeutic processes.

I began weekly massage treatments. Vonnie was so sweet — she even offered a discounted price to cancer patients! I regarded my hour-long therapeutic massage as a wellness appointment and with only one or two exceptions, have never missed my appointments to this day (five years later). Boy, has Vonnie seen me at my worst!

Massage doesn't just feel good. Research shows it reduces the heart rate, increases the blood circulation and lymph flow, relaxes muscles, improves range of motion, increases endorphins (the body's natural pain killers) and more. This was especially beneficial after my double-mastectomy as well. Therapeutic massage definitely helps me feel less anxious and stressed. A writer for the *"Chicago Tribune"* stated, "Massage is to the human body what a tune-up is to an automobile." I will continue to receive therapeutic massage as part of my ongoing wellness program!

Reflexology. In my opinion, the best way to find a qualified and respected therapist is by personal referral. I was fortunate that Vonnie was able to point me in the direction of a wonderful reflexologist. I had continued to do reflexology on myself until I found Paula! Paula was more than a reflexologist to me. She became a wonderful friend! We visited the entire appointment. We shared healthy recipes. We dished on husbands and kids and friends, and most importantly, we prayed together. Like therapeutic massage, I had a standing wellness appointment with Paula every week. Unless the weather was horrific, I showed up without fail. It takes a dedication to wellness to keep all the various weekly appointments, but I knew I could never "fall off the wagon", back into my old routine. After all, my previous lifestyle choices could very likely have played a role in my cancer in the first place, right?

Reflexology is a science that deals with the principle that there are reflexes in the feet and hands relative to each and every organ in the body. By properly working on these reflexes, reflexology can help to relieve many health problems in a natural way. Some form of reflexology was practiced by the Egyptians as early as 2330 BC. Reflexology as we know it, was first researched and developed in America during the 1930's and 1940's. Today, there are thousands of reflexologists practicing all over the world.

In July 2002, John, Colby and I went to Africa. Because of the extended travel time to our destination, I asked the camp to please find a reflexologist so the three of us could receive a treatment. They found a reflexologist who agreed to drive two hours each way to come to our camp and give us reflexology and therapeutic massage treatments! This would be John's first reflexology treatment, and as it turned out, was very timely. During his treatment the reflexologist found a sensitive area on his foot (which ultimately was found to be related to an enlarged adrenal gland). She explained this was most likely due to a high level of stress. She worked the area, but suggested John have a reflexology treatment when we arrived back in the States. A week or so later, John began receiving treatments from my reflexologist, Paula. She too, felt the same spot and concurred that John's level of stress was very high and advised him to have a series of treatments. Gradually, the enlarged spot on his foot went away and today John swears by reflexology!

Reflexology is something I highly recommend for cancer patients as it can also help normalize the body's functions and promote natural healing. It treats the entire body, not just specific organs. It promotes integration of mind and emotions, and helps relieve stress. Many common and serious illnesses are directly linked to stress, and relieving it, allows the body to heal itself naturally.

As a cancer patient, I believe in chemotherapy and surgery (as long as surgery is performed at the proper time as determined by a multi-disciplinary team of physicians, not a surgeon alone). Based on my experience, long-term Stage IV survival rates do not seem to improve when patients adhere solely to Western medicine. Trying non-invasive, drug-free treatments that are potentially very beneficial and have few/ no negative side effects, seems like a no-brainer to me. Incorporating everything possible to increase my odds of long-term survival has become my way of life and in spite of everything I have been through, I have never felt better. I believe reflexology and therapeutic massage have played a key role in my "journey to wellness"!

(As with any complementary or alternative treatment, please consult your physician(s) prior to beginning massage if you have been diagnosed with cancer, especially lymphoma. I was advised by my physician to discontinue yoga when an inexplicable "hot spot" or an area of increased activity/blood flow was detected on a PET scan).

Connie's cancer returned, and after a long, valiantly fought battle, she passed away in October 2002. Sometimes, even if we do everything in our power — everything "right", we are unable to overcome this horrible disease.

Connie is an angel, only now in heaven, and her spirit continues to guide me, even today. Every time I see a feather, I think of her!

Here is a poem I wrote for Connie during the last months of her life, while I was away in Africa.

For My Forever Friend

When I was looking for answers,
I found Connie.
When I need to see a smiling face,
hear words of encouragement and hope,
she is there.

She's taught me everything she knows
and embraces me with open arms;
we share a spirit only few others
could really understand.

She guides me along the way
with calmness and character;
bursting full of energy, love,
compassion and dignity.

Always putting others first,
never uttering an angry word;
with a genuine kindness others only aspire to.

Like the big sister I have never had,
she takes my hand and offers shelter under her wing;
with a desire to protect me,
to ensure my safety.

With the face of an angel,
she calms my fears;
her touch gives me strength…
together, we will win!

We both understand what life is about,
how precious it is;
how thankful we are for it.

We regard each day as a special gift,
and love with every ounce of our being.

Although we're terrified inside,
we both try hard to keep it in;
we want to be tough.

We laugh together,
we cry together;
and we are strong together.

First and foremost devoted wives,
loving mothers, special daughters and sisters but —

ALWAYS, FOREVER FRIENDS!

**December, 2000 – My memory of Connie will never fade.
She passed to a better place in October 2002, but instilled
in me a never-ending strength to fight like hell!**

Chapter 8

The Power of Family & Friends

"When chill winds blow fierce, a friend acts like a torch, guiding you to safety, giving you warmth, comforting you 'til the storm is over."

---Stuart & Linda MacFarlane

Family. What can I say, how much can I say, how can I say it? I will never be able to find the words to show the depth of my love and gratitude for my family's ever-present and unwavering love and support given to me from the day of my diagnosis to this day.

I don't know how I could have survived without the constant support of my husband John. No matter what I wanted to do, what seemingly crazy or unorthodox treatment I proposed to try (and sometimes involve him in), he was ok with it. However, it was when we found a way to work together – on the Touched by Cancer Foundation show homes – that I believe, John found his "voice" to speak out against cancer. He was able to tap his own expertise and put his many years of experience in the homebuilding industry to use in our joint fight against the disease.

My son Colby was only thirteen when I was diagnosed. I continued to drive him to and from school daily, even during my most difficult treatments. I enjoyed our car rides and we talked about everything I was going through. He wanted very much to understand what I was experiencing and feeling, and although he was young, he always wanted to know what he could do to help. He listened to me, and at times, he was my pillar of strength. I think he likely grew up faster than his peers. Now at age 18, his goal is to be a doctor. He witnessed firsthand, the challenges I faced as a cancer patient, and he would now like to be part of the next generation of health care professionals that understands and recognizes the power of combining Western medicine with so-called alternative treatments and complementary modalities. He would like to give of himself in honor of my journey and our sacrifices as a family, in order to help other families that face terminal illnesses. For me, that would give tremendous meaning to all that I have endured, and perhaps offer at least a partial answer to "why did this happen to me?"

Friends. Cancer and friends – for me, both have been a blessing. I realize that to some, it may seem strange to say that cancer has been a blessing — please read on. Just as having and surviving cancer has changed my outlook on life, it has also changed my outlook on friends. Before my diagnosis, I had a wonderful group of friends; after my diagnosis, the true friendships blossomed into deeper, more meaningful relationships. Some friendships became strained and psychologically draining for me, and fell apart, never to be repaired. I understand though — I believe the whole journey is obviously part of God's plan for me. Although I have lost friends, the new and deep friendships I have made are real and true. My friends love me for who I am – they're not afraid of me. They're not worried that they can "catch" cancer from me or something crazy like that. (I do think the uninformed still believe that cancer is a communicable disease – in some ways, we have a long way to go!) I do not believe there are any accidents. A friend once told me, "Everyone is in your life for either a reason, a season or a lifetime." My experience with cancer has shown me which of my long-time friends are truly there for me, and will continue to be there throughout my lifetime; friends like Kathy Davidson, Debbie Morris, Rozanne and Phil Scimeca, Sheila and Vic Zinn, Laura Myer, Linda Lober-Hinds, Cheryl Lewis, Bob and Kendra Wooldridge, David Adams, Craig and Nancy Hamilton — they loved me before cancer, were there for me every step of the way through the diagnosis, the many months of grueling treatments, and to this day. Cancer did not scare them away; unlike some others, it drew many of them even closer to me. I definitely say "I love you" to each of them more often now. Prior to my diagnosis, it was sometimes difficult for me to convey my feelings and emotions, but once I heard the words "you have cancer", the preciousness of life, the love of family, and the meaning of friendship became more evident. It then became so easy to let those I loved know how very important and valued they are.

I also thank God for the special people that came into my life essentially because of my cancer diagnosis: Connie Soden, Brian and Tonya Johnston, Kim Carlos, Katie Harman, Lara Moritz, Paula Miller, Michelle Rierson, Jami and John Hepting, Carol Waldo, Sandra Duncan, Cindy Pederson, Robin Ayers, Josephine LoGuidice, Sheila and Jerry Davis, Lori and Ted Maguire, Carol and Tom Rau, and Joni and Ron Riffle. Although it is possible that our paths may have eventually crossed, I now share a special connection to each of these individuals. They have helped build my faith, and have given me strength and confidence. They have been there for me, each in their own way, and often when I needed it most. They continually reaffirm their belief in me and let me know that I am on the right path. They give me the support I need to stay the course, so that I can continue my daily fight to live in this fantastic life I share with John, Colby, and my wonderful family and friends.

Family and friends are truly what continues to make my world go 'round! I have been fortunate to travel with them, laugh with them and cry with them. Sharing special anniversaries, holidays, momentous birthdays and events with my family and friends, gives me something wonderful to look forward to on a daily basis. Pre-cancer, I, like many others, did not make enough time for special times with loved ones, as often as I should have. Surviving cancer has changed that, and now that time seems as important to me as the air I breathe and the water I drink. I only hope and pray I can give as much to each of them in return!

Chapter 9

The Power of the Touched by Cancer Foundation

"October, 2001. I woke up this morning with so many ideas — ideas that turned into plans that I hope will help so many others better understand cancer and what they can do about it."

I had an idea… I wanted to build a new home and donate our profit from the home to breast cancer research and awareness. Our subcontractors and suppliers had been asking us for over a year what they could do for John and me. Besides continuing with their prayers, this was the answer: we can use our own knowledge and resources to build a house to raise money for cancer causes! Of course the first person I approached to discuss my idea, was John. I believe he saw a spark in my eyes for the first time in eighteen months.

I had just become truly confident that I was not going to die, and I needed to follow through with my promises to God: each time I was scanned or x-rayed, I asked God to, "please spare me; please let me live and in return I promise to do whatever I can to help others with their fight." This was the answer and the vehicle with which to follow through with my promises!

John seemed interested in the idea. I think he thought that having this new "baby" in my life would also help to relieve the sadness I felt for not being able to have the child we were hoping to have together, when I was diagnosed with cancer. The show home would, in fact, be my baby.

My friends embraced the idea and started falling into place to form the committees. Lara Moritz, our Kansas City, Missouri ABC television anchor, agreed to be our local spokesperson. The mayor of Kansas City, Missouri also embraced the idea along with other local politicians who liked the idea of a local, grass-roots effort trying to make a real and meaningful difference in the battle against cancer. In addition, although many people told me I was crazy to ask, while still in her reign as Miss America 2002, Katie Harman, agreed to attend the ribbon-cutting ceremony and also help to convey the Foundation's message of hope and awareness on a national level! This was important to me, not only because someone of such prominence was interested in getting involved with my brand new idea, but also because Katie's major platform and campaign as Miss America was to spread the message about the meaning of a "metastatic breast cancer" diagnosis. I had been trying to teach everyone I knew since April of 2000 what it meant to have "metastatic breast cancer", so it was very significant that Katie Harman was already spreading this message nationally!

Together, John and I sought the help of many other dedicated individuals to help us get things organized, far too many to cite individually in these few, short pages. So many people desire to "give back" in any way they can; someone just needs to hold their hand and guide them along! At this point, God was clearly guiding me because this little "baby" was quickly growing into much more responsibility than I could ever handle on my own!

I was first advised by a childhood friend to start a 501(c)(3) foundation. I had never even heard of something like that before; unless it had to do with selling or building new homes, I felt like an idiot! However, as I did more research about the subject, I realized that the home would serve as the "foundation" (no pun intended!) of the not-for-profit foundation. It would be not only the Foundation's major source of fundraising (by selling the home to interested buyers and then donating the net profits of the home's proceeds to cancer-related causes), but also a vehicle by which to convey a message of hope and education to others newly diagnosed. Beyond knowing that the home could serve this main purpose, I knew little else how to make things happen the "right" way, legally, morally and purposely. In order to accomplish the feats that lay ahead, I knew I would need help.

That's when God sent me another angel to help with the task. I knew when I met Brian Johnston, a Kansas City attorney, there was immediately a connection. We had both been "touched by cancer" way too many times and he was spiritually searching for a way to "give back" in memory of loved ones who had lost their fight to cancer. Brian took the lead, set up the foundation with the state, created its by-laws, prepared and filed the necessary paperwork with the Internal Revenue Service to start the process of securing "501(c)(3)" status for the foundation. (As a footnote to anyone that thinks of starting a foundation and believes that getting the necessary IRS approval is easy, *it isn't*: it is a very time-intensive process that takes several months to get approved and requires the help of people that know what they are doing to get it done right!). Brian not only got us started, but also continues today serving as Chairman of the Board of Directors.

I cannot stress how important it is for each new foundation to have a "Brian". I know I would have thrown my hands up many times throughout the last three years if not for his energy, drive and commitment to the Foundation. Although Brian told me in the very beginning how much work it would be to start a non-profit foundation that relies solely upon the efforts and energies of volunteers to accomplish its purposes, I never dreamed it would be so much work. There are constant pressures to do your very best in raising funds to support the Foundation's purposes and causes, but always the requirement to do so in a manner that is allowable by approved IRS guidelines. In addition, there are constant struggles to make sure there are enough volunteers to support the Foundation's efforts, while at the same time not too heavily taxing the relationships of friends and family to make things happen. Brian has always been there to help me keep our ultimate priorities straight: to spread the messages of hope and healing that we *know* are helping save lives for tomorrow that could not be saved yesterday based on the lack of knowledge of cancer treatment options and alternatives.

The Touched by Cancer Foundation was created on January 24, 2002 (we originally organized as the Lori C. Lober Cancer Foundation, but later changed the name because we soon realized how many people have been "touched by cancer" in their lives, through themselves, a loved one or close family member or friend) and today exists, "to become a comprehensive resource to increase cancer awareness and promote positive treatment outcomes." We strive to accomplish this mission by:

- Educating newly diagnosed cancer patients about multiple opinions and correct diagnosis *before* treatment begins (for example, it is particularly important to not pursue surgical removal or other surgical options until you know this is the absolute best alternative available);
- Creating awareness of "comprehensive cancer centers" (e.g., M.D. Anderson, in Houston, TX, Duke University, in Durham, NC, or you may contact the National Cancer Institute to find other comprehensive cancer center locations throughout the country) ;
- Providing information to the community regarding all treatment options (e.g. clinical trials, Eastern & Western medicine in combination and complementary modalities); and,
- Promoting overall health and wellness to those diagnosed with cancer or any other "at risk" individuals.

We have now passed our third year anniversary and continue to make strides forward in accomplishment of our ultimate goal of ensuring that anyone diagnosed with cancer is fully equipped with the information they need to fight and win their battle against cancer. We've had very dedicated Board members (again, too many to name but we wouldn't be where we are without our past Board members, including my brother Larry Wittmeyer, Kim Carlos, and John Hennessy, along with our current Board, including John Lober, Sandra Duncan, Sheila Davis and Josephine LoGiudice), and many volunteers to help us get where we are. However, we've still got miles to go before we finish!

In the fulfillment of our mission, we've now built three homes dedicated to the purposes and causes of the Foundation. The nation's first-ever "BUILDING FOR A CURE DESIGNER SHOW HOME" was completed by Provence Homes, Inc., by John Lober, in October, 2002. The funds raised were used to create awareness through the sponsorship of several cancer-related events held at the home during Breast Cancer Awareness Month. In addition, the proceeds raised from the sale of the home were also distributed to the University of Kansas School of Medicine (to support Dr. Carol Fabian's Flaxseed Study as an alternative to traditional chemotherapy approaches in breast cancer patients), and the University of Missouri at Kansas City's School of Medicine (to support the establishment of a new comprehensive cancer center).

Local Kansas City businesses and interior designers decorated the home to provide a unique "show home" décor that encouraged the attendance of many who knew nothing about our new Foundation or its cancer-related purposes. In addition, many subcontractors and suppliers to the home donated their time and products for the home so that the net profits from the sale of the home provide even more funds to support the Foundation's cancer-related causes.

Not only were visitors allowed to view the outstanding home (that was also featured in several local and national publications and awarded several local awards for its design and purposes) they also received valuable information about cancer and available treatment options. In particular, the Foundation supplied an informative publication that conveyed useful information regarding breast cancer and the importance of early diagnosis.

In May of 2004, we completed a second show home, also built by Provence Homes, Inc. by John Lober and now referred to as the "Building Awareness Designer Show Home", and held additional cancer-related events that focused on health, wellness, and healing. The 2004 home had a consistent decorative style and theme that highlighted the cancer battles of several prominent cancer survivors and celebrities, with additional information being made available that discussed each person's type of cancer and the available treatment options. In addition, due to the popularity of the home and its events, the 2004 Show Home was sold within three weeks of its first public event! The proceeds from the 2004 Show Home have now supported additional contributions to other worthy causes, including M.D. Anderson's House of Wellness, and Turning Point of Kansas City's Center for Hope and Healing.

The Foundation has now completed its third Building Awareness Designer Show Home, which opened to the public in August, 2005. The significance of the 2005 Show Home is not only its importance in raising funds, and in spreading the Foundation's educational campaign and message to a new audience, but also because it is the first home that has been built without the help and assistance of John or myself. A prominent Kansas City homebuilder, Tom French Construction, Inc., built the 2005 show home in Lenexa, Kansas. Both Tom and his wife Gayle, have taken the Foundation's mission and made it their own! This is an important first step as we move to our next goal, which is to take the Building Awareness Designer

Show Home model outside the Kansas City area, to spread our messages of awareness, hope and healing throughout the nation. It is our goal that homebuilders across the nation will continue to embrace our ideas and concepts to initiate similar events each and every year until cancer is torn down and demolished from our existence.

While the show home continues to serve as the Foundation's "main event", we also strive to incorporate other means that can serve as an outlet in which to convey its messages. One of these additional outlets is through the Foundation's sponsorship of Friperie, a unique resale boutique, which opened in April, 2003 and is located in Olathe, Kansas. Through media campaigns and general word of mouth, this French-inspired boutique is already known in Kansas City as a great location to donate and purchase "gently worn" apparel and home décor items, but also more importantly as an outreach that provides daily education and support of cancer-related concerns. Friperie is also the exclusive outlet for a unique line of all-natural aromatherapy and bath products. Friperie differs from other non-profit resale shops because it includes additional education efforts, mainly through wellness seminars. These are offered to the public free of charge, and discuss topics such as The Importance of Drinking Green Tea, Proper Nutrition for Optimal Wellness, and The Importance of Reflexology. There is a team of more than twenty volunteers running Friperie, most of whom have been "touched by cancer". Working at the store is their way of "giving back" in honor of lost loved ones. All profits raised from the resale of goods are provided to the Foundation to support its mission and goals.

In addition, the Foundation sponsors other fund-raising events in Kansas City including annual golf and tennis tournaments, and an annual black-tie gala, and participates in other local organizations' cancer and health and wellness-related educational and fund-raising events.

The Touched by Cancer Foundation has truly been a labor of love, and has ultimately helped me focus on helping others. It has become a vehicle through which I can touch other lives and "give back". Each time I tell my story I am encouraged to stay on my long-term path to wellness. It's not just about going through the motions; having surgery, having chemotherapy, being tested, going to doctors' appointments, day in and day out. There is so much more to it. Eating correctly, continuing on my journey of overall optimal health and wellness, living each day to the fullest, enjoying my friends and family like I never did "before cancer" is what I am about now and what I intend to be about for many, many years to come! The Touched by Cancer Foundation truly helps me fulfill my purpose and meaning in life.

Conclusion

In July, 2003, I met with my oncologist. This had come to be a somewhat "normal" occurrence. But now, visiting M.D. Anderson Cancer Center merely to obtain information for this book, was both a strange and wonderful feeling. This was the first time I flew to Houston without anticipating being examined, X-rayed, poked, and prodded! I was there for a new cause – this book - which, for me is yet another revelation that my cancer journey happened for a reason.

My doctors cannot give me definite answers as to why my treatments have been successful when others have failed, or even why I'm alive. However, they have said many times that I am a "very proactive patient." Of course, being proactive does not guarantee success and long-term survival – unfortunately, there are no guarantees. However, I feel that truly believing that I was not going to die, most certainly was an important factor. In addition to that, my faith, the support of my family and friends, the combination of everything discussed in this book, and yes, a little luck, I believe all contributed to my long-term survival. Prior to being diagnosed with cancer, I would not necessarily have considered myself an extraordinarily lucky person. Now, however, the quality of life I live every day is much richer, the special moments more memorable, and the love I have to offer both to myself as well as to others, is deeper and more fulfilling. This is precisely why I tell people I feel "blessed" to have actually had cancer, and deeply grateful to now be healthy and happy.

Appendices

My Journey

<u>11/29/95</u>
First mammogram – "Dense breasts with micro calcifications-no cancer".

<u>1998</u>
Second mammogram – 11/20/98 – negative for cancer; appointment with OB/GYN – one suspicious area
Appointment with first surgeon – would need a biopsy to rule out cancer – thought the suspicious area was "probably not cancer". Sought second opinion.
Two appointments with second surgeon – No need for biopsy, it was "fibrous dysplasia; nothing to worry about."

<u>April 10, 2000</u>
Third mammogram – negative for cancer – I felt something was not right.

<u>April 13, 2000</u>
First appointment with third surgeon – first biopsy – indicated I had "Ductal Carcinoma in situ".

<u>April 20, 2000</u>
Second appointment with third surgeon – Second biopsy (to rule out inflammatory breast cancer).

<u>April 24, 2000</u>
First appointment with Oncologist at M.D. Anderson Cancer Center in Houston, Texas.

<u>April 24-28, 2000</u>
Ongoing testing to determine "stage". 7 cm. x 4 cm. breast tumor confirmed. Positive nodes revealed during fine needle aspiration. Inflammatory breast cancer ruled out via core biopsies. CT scan positive for liver metastasis. Meetings with breast cancer multi-disciplinary team of doctors at MDACC.

<u>April 28, 2000</u>
Diagnosis of Stage IV breast cancer with metastatis (spreading) to the liver – THE WORST DAY OF MY LIFE.

May 1, 2000
Surgical insertion of first catheter and first chemotherapy treatment
at MDACC – Taxotere/Herceptin clinical trial paperwork signed;
treatment begins.

May, 2000
My brother Lance, passes away of cancer. I fight to live in honor of him.
Had it not been for Lance, I would not know that comprehensive cancer
centers exist; something I wish we had learned years earlier to aid him in
his fight.

June, July, August, 2000
Taxotere/Herceptin chemotherapy continues.

September 28, 2000
Liver surgery at MDACC – experimental Radio Frequency Ablation
– believed by my multi-disciplinary team to be successful!

October, 2000
More chemotherapy – Taxotere/Herceptin.

November 10, 2000
Double mastectomy – MDACC – no reconstruction.

Thanksgiving, 2000
On vacation with my mother and Colby in Cabo San Lucas
recuperating from the two surgeries. (I believe "getting away from it all"
can be very healing!)

December, 2000
More chemotherapy – Taxotere/Herceptin.

January 1, 2001
Dateline television program featuring "metastatic breast cancer guru"
Dr. Yeshi Dhonden.

January, February, March, 2001
Adriamycin, Cytoxin, 5-FU Regime.

Summer/Fall, 2001
Navelbene Experimental Chemotherapy Regime – (I was scared to
quit!).

Spring, 2002
DUKE University Immunization Study in North Carolina – involved 6 trips to Durham, NC.

Summer, 2002
Double doses of Herceptin every 21 days begin.

Summer, 2002 to October, 2005
Herceptin continues. Reflexology treatments, therapeutic massage, colonics, acupuncture, chiropractic alignment, proper nutrition, herbal supplementation and Tibetan herbs continue. Appointments with Dr. Yeshi Dhonden every six months; re-evaluation and follow-up. Although PET scans show a "hot spot" at my left hip area, I continue to thrive. I am medically diagnosed as "no evidence of disease". I continue on-going bone scans, PET scans, x-rays, echo-cardiogram studies, etc. every three to six months. I strive to eliminate daily stress (the main thing doctors say can cause the cancer to quickly and aggressively return).

Resources

CANCER
National Cancer Institute (NCI)
NCI Public Inquiries Office
6116 Executive Boulevard, Room 3036A
Bethesda, MD 20892-8322
1-800-4-CANCER
www.cancer.gov
www.nci.nih.gov

Oncolink Editorial Board
Abramson Cancer Center of the University of Pennsylvania
3400 Spruce Street – 2 Donner
Philadelphia, PA 19104-4283
Fax: 215-349-5445
www.oncolink.org

American Cancer Society
1-800-ACS-2345
www.cancer.org

COMPLEMENTARY AND ALTERNATIVE MEDICINE
National Institutes of Health
National Center for Complementary and Alternative Medicine
6707 Democracy Boulevard, Suite 401
Bethesda, MD 20892-5475
(888) 644-6226
www.chid.nih.gov

ACUPUNCTURE
American Academy of Medical Acupuncture
5820 Wilshire Boulevard
Los Angeles, CA 90036
213-937-5514
www.medicalacupuncture.org

American Association of Oriental Medicine
433 Front Street
Catasqua, PA 18032
610-266-1433
www.aaom.org

HOLISTIC MEDICINE
American Holistic Health Association
P.O. Box 17400
Anaheim, CA 92817
714-779-6152
www.ahha.org

American Holistic Medical Association
6728 Old McLean Village Drive
McLean, VA 22101
703-556-9728
www.holisticmedicine.org

REFLEXOLOGY
International Institute of Reflexology
P.O. Box 12462
St. Petersburg, FL 33733
813-343-4811
www.reflexology-usa.net

THERAPEUTIC TOUCH
Nurse Healers Professional Associates
1211 Locust Street
Philadelphia, PA 19107
215-545-8079
www.therapeutic-touch.org

COLON THERAPY
International Association for Colon Hydrotherapy
P.O. Box 461285
San Antonio, TX 78246
210-366-2888
www.iact@healthy.net

Dedications and Remembrances

I have found that so many people I talk with have a strong desire —
a strong *need*, to express their feelings about how cancer has impacted
their lives and the lives of family members, friends, and even casual
acquaintances. The following "dedications and remembrances" are a
collection of responses from a number of individuals, wanting to do
just that. They are honest, heartfelt, and very touching words and I
am honored to give voice to them in the pages of this book. LL

*"The journey of loving someone diagnosed with cancer changes your
life forever. The daily battles with the illness are mind-boggling. However,
'Can'cer is an opportunity to be a beacon of light, of hope, of strength, and
persistence to live life to its fullest each and every day. My siblings were both
diagnosed with cancer and I personally think about their diagnoses every day.
Lori is a wonderful, inspirational woman with a giving heart and a positive
attitude. Lance's memory brings a smile to my face and it is the knowledge of
his strength, his humor and his goodness that inspire me to be the person I am.
He lives through me every day. Cancer has helped me realize that good health,
happiness, the hope of tomorrow, and the support of family and friends are gifts
from God. I feel truly blessed."*

           - Larry E. Wittmeyer, Jr.

*"In memory of my brother, John Wooldridge and my father, Robert; both
lost their battle with cancer. I was too young to really understand my father's
illness, and yet always there with my brother on his trying journey of hope,
treatment and then sad reality. John's cancer gave us time to share, to express
our love for each other, and a chance to say goodbye. Without a desperately
needed cure, it took away so much more . . . my best friend."*

           - Bob Wooldridge

"I came to know Barbara Phillips in 1999 when her battle with cancer had already begun. Her positive outlook on life was contagious. I spent time with her every week but she would not allow the focus of our conversations to be about her --- her life was about her family and friends. She taught me that there is always laughter, light and love to be enjoyed. Barbara did not lose her life to cancer December 31, 2003, only her body. I will never forget her."

- Paula Miller

"Anita Dube was my mother's younger sister, who passed away from cancer at the tender age of 19. My mother's family has long been plagued by cancer, as she also lost her father and mother to this disease. I am happy to say that her brother, my Uncle Dave is a cancer-free survivor! Anita has been gone for a long time now, but not forgotten by her family, and her spirit lives on in her namesake, my younger sister, Anita, and her daughter, Alexa."

- Sandra Duncan

"In Memory of my uncle, Don Feeback:
Several family members and friends, both survivors and non-survivors of cancer, have played a part in how I have changed my lifestyle. Good eating habits, exercise, hard work, and laughter are now a part of my typical day and I also try not to stress about things over which I have no control."

- Sheila K. Zinn

"In honor of Kay Moritz: My mom continues to be my mentor. She never faltered during her battle with breast cancer. Cancer did not change her, it only made her stronger! An inspiration, she teaches me to know myself and believe in God's plan."

- Lara Moritz

"My friend since kindergarten, Lori Lober has shown over the years how generous, hard-working, funny and giving she is. She is beautiful inside and out. Lori has been an inspiration throughout her cancer journey. She has taught me not to give up, to help others and to remain positive. I know she has beaten this terrible disease because of her devotion to wellness – she understands the need to stay focused on her health – and because of her optimism in the face of adversity."

- Kathy M. Davidson

"In Memory of My Mom:

My mom was used to controlling everything. Cancer was the first thing that controlled her. As I watched my mom slowly slip away from a disease that neither she nor I could control, I too suffered an inconsolable experience that will haunt me forever. To those who are working to control, if not eliminate, cancer's reach, thank you for providing me and many others with hope."

- Tonya Johnston

"My friend Carol Wrobel is truly an inspiration. After being diagnosed with breast cancer, Carol provided the same extraordinary level of care and devotion to her family and friends as always. While caring for herself and enduring the difficult cancer treatments, she guided her daughter through high school graduation and the college entry process and still managed to throw her a party to remember! She continued to care for her ailing parents and maintain a loving home where all are welcome. May the love, comfort and acceptance she showers upon others, be returned to her tenfold."

- Sandra Duncan

"Herman Peter: You inspired so many during your life with your amazing attitude. No one ever knew you as a "blind man", because you lived life to the fullest. Nothing stopped you - not even the subways of New York City! Your battle with cancer was the same — you never gave up. You are sadly missed by our family, but never forgotten."

- Lorraine Hightower

"In Memory of my Grandfather:

My grandfather's cancer diagnosis forced him to allow others to care for him. That was perhaps more difficult than the pain he endured. He treated people with respect throughout his life."

- Lori Robben

"To My Heroes:

My two greatest heroes were taken from me by cancer. They both came to me at different times in my life when I needed help the most. My first hero was my grandfather Doug Waldo, who basically served as my father (when my natural father left my sister and me). He was there for me as a strong male role model and friend, and I loved him dearly. He fought "the good fight", but lost his battle against cancer after six years. My other hero was my step-dad, Frank Barnes, who "took over" for my grandfather after his passing. He too, loved me as a father and a friend. He was a great listener and a real friend to me. He also fought hard, but lost his battle with the disease after five years. I loved both of these men. The fight each made, and the positive attitude each man had, has changed my life forever".

- Fritz Waldo

"In remembrance of my beautiful grandmother, Lora Elizabeth Mesker, who did not survive her battle against colon cancer. Her spirit lives on through my work helping others achieve better health and preventative care. I dedicate my career as a health care practitioner to her, my Uncle Ron, who lost his fight against Leukemia, my mother Phyllis Cawrey, who to date, has accomplished three twenty-six mile marathons to raise funds for cancer research, and to my dear friend, Lori Lober, who is an inspiration to me".

- With love,
Caroline Elizabeth Cawrey

"Jane Nicholson was a wonderful woman who spent her entire life helping others. Always putting others' needs before her own, she left a long legacy of charity and kindness behind, as well as love and compassion within her family. She loved to garden and manage the gift-shop in the local hospital, all in her free time. After fighting a year-long battle against pancreatic cancer, she joined God, so she could watch over her family in her own way. We know lovingly, that if Heaven didn't have a gift shop, it does now, and Jane is running it! Every time I see a flower, I know it's from her, and her garden of love can bloom more brilliantly, especially her yellow roses! I love you Nani!"

- Susie Nicholson

"Dick Wilson represented what the sport of diving is all about: the kids, the divers, and the sport. Dick believed anyone could be a champion and always had something positive to say. He was much more than a coach – he was more like a father figure. Dick fought throat cancer and when God made his final call, he just smiled, and decided it was time to go. Dick was an inspiration to us all and will be missed by his family and everyone who knew him. He is now in a much better place, in peace, and without pain. All divers are now surely to have a guardian angel on their shoulders. Thank you 'Coach' for teaching me to never give up!"

- Susie Nicholson

"Just last month I was touched by cancer in the most personal way. My father-in-law was diagnosed with cancer (of the mouth) only two months before his 92nd birthday. I have known people who have survived cancer, and many who have not, but they were further removed — the wife of a friend, a distant uncle or cousin. I had not realized how many people whose lives connect in some way with my own, fight this horrible disease every day. After learning all the facts, we have decided as a family, that aggressive treatment in our case is not a viable option, but my wife and I are proud to participate in the Touched by Cancer Foundation, and feel we have found a new family to share our deepest fears with, along with our best wishes. We love you Ben — your life has been an inspiration for us all!"

- Andy Robson

"Murlan, you touched so many hearts with your kind spirit. Although you are no longer here with us, your spirit will forever live in the wonderful memories you have given to Mom, Jami, Landon and me. You will not be forgotten."

- Jody Beynon

"In memory of my mother, Emili Mae Blaha, who lived 47 years filled with strength, vitality, and love. Here are her words:

How have I coped with this struggle in my life? My answer, (and I will take the liberty to say the same answer would be given by my family, friends and doctors), is that I have coped physically and emotionally, very well. The human spirit can overcome many obstacles in life if the circumstances of our lives can be balanced with good times along with bad times. Those good times can come at many moments. While in intensive care and physically very critical, a friend spent the night on a cot next to my bed. She had given me a massage, tucked me into my comfortable nest, which consisted of two blankets, six pillows and a box of tissue. I closed my eyes but couldn't fall asleep. When I opened my eyes, I found my friend staring down at me. I had no voice, but I motioned for her to close her eyes and go to sleep. She said she was afraid to fall asleep because I might need her and because I couldn't talk, she was worried she wouldn't hear me. We both fell asleep after she moved her cot to a position where she could hold my hand and I could squeeze if I needed her. Love and support is what brings us through tough times. Those moments give balance to trauma. The people who surround a cancer patient can help in so many ways."

- Laura McCabe

"So often you see the attributes of a parent in their child... especially the treasured qualities that set them apart and make them shine. In the case of my husband Tim, I can see so much of his mother Kathleen, in him. Kathleen left this world for a much better place on September 24, 1997 after a courageous eleven-year battle with cancer. I was never fortunate enough to meet her in her lifetime, but am privileged to see her legacy in her extraordinary son, and now feel as if I truly have met her.

Kathleen was passionate about life and loved her family with all her heart. Always ready to have fun, she was the type of mother who would sit in the backseat of the family van next to her other two children during vacations, and throw spit wads at Tim and his father in the front, laughing hysterically at the reactions she'd then receive! She loved to fish alongside her adventurous sons, shop for hours with her beautiful daughter, and stand proudly beside her husband, a Chief in the Air National Guard. She encouraged all she met to reach for their dreams as well as appreciate every precious moment.

Kathleen Ebner's life is a true testament to the power of a legacy, and I feel honored to watch her legacy continue to touch so many lives...mine included."

- Katie Harman Ebner

"I would like to remember Sandi Vaccaro. She was a beautiful woman I met at my first chemo treatment. Her calm demeanor and warm smile got me through my first treatment. She talked me through the whole thing, and before I knew it, I was done. Her grace, dignity and courage, inspired me to be and to do the same. Sadly for us, Sandi lost her battle with cancer, but I will never forget her. I think of her often and smile, knowing she was my angel on earth and is now my angel in heaven."

- Carol Rau

"We will always remember John L. Ayers as a loving father, a brave soldier, and a gentle soul who lost his battle with cancer. He was born on Christmas Day, December 25, 1930, and died at the age of 65 on Easter, April 7, 1996. He served proudly as a Sergeant in the U.S. Army during the Korean War. He was a home-town boy at heart and lived in Brownsburg, Indiana, where he enjoyed his family and friends. We know he is watching over us and we miss him dearly."

- Jordan, Robin & Taylor Ayers

"I want to thank God for allowing me to know two people: Mildred Jones and Connie Soden. They taught me how to live with words of wisdom, love, friendship and encouragement. They taught me how to die without fear and how to die with hope, love and a greater expectation than we have here on earth."

- Vonnie Niederwimmer

"My wife Carol's battle with breast cancer showed how strong she is and how much love we share together. It was a period in our lives we will cherish; it was a growing experience. Her positive attitude helped those around her deal with their own struggles. She helped other patients cope with the anguish and doubts they had in dealing with this disease. I watched how she dealt with the chemo and radiation sessions — she was truly inspirational. She is my life and my love forever!"

- Tom Rau

"Cancer has touched many people around me, including some very special family members:

To Lori: You are definitely the strongest person cancer has had to battle… congrats on never letting it get the best of you. You are an inspiration.

To my Dad: I know it was very unexpected, but you have fared well and it has taught you to care for yourself and to never take anything for granted, like eating.

To Linda: Keep your head up and live life to its fullest.

I love you all and am very proud of your strength in fighting this horrible disease."

- Shelley Bringolf Lober

"In memory of Max Kruse:

It seems like things in life go by so fast – I had just spoken to Max about having coffee a short while ago, believing he was going to beat his cancer. I regret that I was unable to follow up with him. He was an extremely strong willed and intelligent man who helped me to look at things in a different light, and I will miss him greatly."

- Robert Jackson

"In memory of Arlene Brownsberger Hunzeker who suffered with cancer for years in the early 70's. If only there were more people like Lori then, working to fight this terrible disease, many of our loved ones might be here to help her today."

- Nancy Krohn

"In loving remembrance of my wonderful grandmother, Clara Ann Haag. Diagnosed with lymphoma late in life, she fought it with a quiet strength that I'll never forget. Memories of her make me smile and inspire me still. While she may not be with me on this earth, she is always with me in spirit.

Also in loving remembrance of "Grandma" Shirley Hoffa who passed away last year after a very long and difficult struggle with cancer. She was an inspiration, a true fighter to the end, and is dearly missed.

Lastly, a dedication to my uncle, Tony Tremmel, who was recently diagnosed with cancer: May God bless you and give you strength. We are all with you through this to support you in whatever way you need. If I could carry the burden for you, I would in a heartbeat. Love you!"

- Michelle Haag Rierson

"When I heard, "Linda we have the results. You have Non-Hodgkins Lymphoma," I was on my cell phone in my car, and although I felt very light-headed, I took a deep breath and said to myself, "Ok. What should I do now?" Because someone very close to me who was diagnosed with cancer, given 18 months to live, refused to believe that, and then fought and won, I knew I had not just received a death sentence. I knew that I too had to take charge, look at all my options, and fight. I am confident that I made the right decision to go to M.D. Anderson Cancer Center in Houston, Texas, where I received what I believe was the best treatment for my condition. The diagnosis made there was more precise than what I had received elsewhere. My sister-in-law Lori Lober was my inspiration. Russ and I thank you Lori from the bottom of our hearts."

- Linda Lober Hinds

Printed in Great Britain
by Amazon.co.uk, Ltd.,
Marston Gate.